NINETEEN BISHOPS
OF THE
EVANGELICAL UNITED BRETHREN CHURCH

Bishops A. R. Clippinger and John S. Stamm shaking hands on November 16, 1946, at the official uniting of the Evangelical and United Brethren churches.

NINETEEN BISHOPS

of the

Evangelical

United Brethren Church

By

PAUL W. MILHOUSE

NINETEEN BISHOPS
OF THE
EVANGELICAL UNITED BRETHREN CHURCH

Copyright © 1974 by Paul W. Milhouse

Manufactured by The Parthenon Press
at Nashville, Tennessee
United States of America

DEDICATED TO
my wife, Mary Frances,
without whose cooperation
this could not have been written

FOREWORD

A church reflects the faith of its leaders. The men whom you will meet on these pages served as bishops in the Evangelical United Brethren Church which is now a part of the United Methodist Church.

Personal association across the years with each of these leaders has strengthened my Christian faith, broadened my understanding of the church and enriched my life. I want you to know them as I have known them—men of faith dedicated to serving God through their church. They are presented in order of their election to the episcopacy.

My sincere thanks and appreciation go to all who assisted in gathering information and to Bishop J. Gordon Howard who volunteered to summarize my ministry in order to make the record complete; to Mrs. Doyle Thorp, my secretary, who typed and retyped notes and manuscripts; and to Frances, my wife, who, as in times past, demonstrated great patience and support during the long period required for research and writing that literally "took over" our leisure time together for many months.

Paul W. Milhouse

CONTENTS

BISHOP A. R. CLIPPINGER

1

Don't Buy Your Coal
Before Conference

A pastor greeted Bishop A. R. Clippinger at the opening session of the fall annual conference by telling him:"I have filled my coal bin for next winter." The bishop, knowing this was a manuever to avoid assignment to another church, replied, "Brother, don't buy your coal before conference next year."

Bishop Clippinger could be firm when he thought it necessary but was known across the church for his fairness in appointments and good judgment as a church executive. A pastor who served under his episcopal leadership for 30 years, said, "He was our spiritual father and I always went to him for advice. He was a man of good judgment."[1] A banker of Dayton, Ohio, where the bishop had his residence from 1910 until his death in 1958, remarked that "He was the only minister whose business judgment I respected."[2] An attorney described him as "a good administrator and a wise counselor."[3] A pastor said he was "a firm but considerate administrator and parliamentarian, at his best when presiding over an annual conference."[4]

Arthur Raymond Clippinger was born September 3, 1878, in Lurgan Township, Franklin County, Pennsylvania, the son of Harry Rankin and Harriet Rebecca Gillan Clippinger.[5] His father, whose ancestors came to America from Germany in 1737, was a farmer for many years and then moved to Shippensburg, Pennsylvania, where he became known as a very meticulous and fine cabinet maker.[6] His mother was of Scotch-Irish descent. "The name Clippinger is synonymous with solidarity of character. All have been stalwart and earnest Christians, each serving in his own characteristic manner and place."[7]

At the age of seven, Arthur knelt at the altar of the Hopewell United Brethren log church house and dedicated his life to God. He was teaching a Sunday school class by the time he was sixteen and was elected superintendent when only eighteen years of age.

After completing the elementary grades in Franklin County, he attended summer classes at Orrstown to qualify for a teaching certificate. After four years of teaching, he borrowed money from the father of one of his pupils to enroll in Lebanon Valley College. During the summer months, he sold Chautauqua drawing boards and writing desks in order to continue in college. He was graduated in 1905.[8]

While a student in Lebanon Valley College, Pennsylvania

Conference granted him probationary membership on October 18, 1903. Before entering his senior year, he served six months as pastor in Greencastle. Before completion of his senior year, he was appointed to New Cumberland, where he continued to serve for two more years, leading the congregation in the erection of a new building.

On October 16, 1907, he and Ellen Weinland Mills were married by her father, Bishop J. S. Mills, in the Mills' home in Annville, Pennsylvania. Immediately following their marriage, the young couple went to New Haven, Connecticut, and Arthur enrolled in the Divinity School of Yale University.[9] While there, he served Congregational churches, but upon graduation in 1910 was appointed pastor of Summit Street United Brethren Church in Dayton, Ohio. He served here eight years and led the congregation in erecting a new building at a new location on Euclid Avenue.

In 1918, he was elected superintendent of the Miami Conference.[10] On May 18, 1921, the United Brethren Church General Conference elected him bishop. Upon presentation to the conference, Bishop Clippinger said: "This should be a time for prayer rather than a time for speech-making. But I would not be true to myself, nor would I be true to you if I did not . . . express my appreciation of the honor which you have conferred upon me . . . . I was brought up in a United Brethren home. Every drop of blood that courses through my veins is United Brethren blood. . . . I wish those pious parents of mine were here in person that I might crown them with some of the honor that you have bestowed upon me."[11]

Bishop Clippinger paid tribute to one of his boyhood pastors, the Reverend James Weidler, calling him a "man of God, not a great preacher, but a man of clean life, of high ideals and noble ambitions." He spoke of his father-in-law as "my ideal in executive ability, also in studious habits." He asked Dr. A. R. Ayres, who signed his first license to preach, and Bishop Washinger, who appointed him to his first charge, to stand beside him and pray for him.[12]

Bishop Clippinger was a strong influence in bringing the Evangelical Church and the United Brethren Church together to form the Evangelical United Brethren Church in 1946. He attended every meeting of the Commission on Union and read

13

the declaration of union at the uniting conference. He was the honored senior bishop of the new church until his retirement in 1950.

His strong leadership was recognized by Lebanon Valley College in 1916 by granting him an honorary Doctor of Divinity degree. The same school honored him again in 1940 with a Doctor of Laws degree.

Bishop Clippinger worked for a strong ministerial pension plan for his church long before such plans were generally accepted.[13] He served on the National Chaplains' Commission during World War II and led in forward looking programs in every phase of church life. He was at the first meeting of the Federal Council of Churches in 1925.[14]

Requesting retirement in 1950, he said: "I lay down my official duties with only one regret; namely, that I have not been able to do more and better work for God and my church. My paternal grandparents and my maternal grandparents were church people. My father and mother . . . were Christian at heart and churchly in practice. They feared God and loved their children . . . . The Bible was read and prayer was heard. Sunday was a day of rest and worship . . . . In a home like that, Mrs. Clippinger and I have brought up three sons . . . . "[15]

Bishop Clippinger left his imprint on many boards and agencies of the church. He visited mission fields in Japan, China, Philippines, Puerto and Santo Domingo, and represented his church at the constituting assembly of the World Council of Churches in Amsterdam in 1948.

Mrs. Clippinger, who could read Latin, Greek, French and German, as well as English, was a great reader of history and biography. Somewhat shy and retiring, she felt her greatest opportunity of service was in the home, but she was also active in charitable and religious organizations of the community. In her own quiet way, she helped many needy people, especially during the days of the great depression of the thirties.[16]

Mrs. Clippinger died June 3, 1955, and the funeral services were conducted from Euclid Avenue Church in Dayton, Ohio, on June 6 with interment in Memorial Park Cemetery.[17]

Bishop Clippinger suffered a stroke while eating lunch in Dayton, Ohio, July 17, 1958. He was attending a meeting of the Board of Bishops. Death came the following morning, just 47 days before his 80th birthday. Funeral services were conducted on July 21 by Bishop George E. Epp from the Euclid Avenue Evangelical United Brethren Church which had been built while he was pastor. His body was laid beside his wife's in Memorial Park.[18]

Bishop Clippinger was a wise counselor and a dedicated servant of the church who served with dignity and devotion.

NOTES

1. Personal correspondence from Dr. John A. Clippenger to the author (January 3, 1973).
2. Ibid.
3. Personal correspondence from Dr. L. L. Huffman to the author (January 29, 1973).
4. Personal correspondence from Dr. Millard J. Miller to the author (January 2, 1973).
5. Personal correspondence from Miss Florence E. Clippinger to the author (October 11, 1972).
6. Personal correspondence from Dr. Conrad K. Clippinger to the author (January 3, 1973).
7. Koontz and Roush, *The Bishops* (Dayton, Ohio: Otterbein Press, 1950), p. 254.
8. Personal correspondence from Miss Florence E. Clippinger to the author (October 11, 1972).
9. Koontz and Roush, *The Bishops*, pp. 255-257.
10. Ibid., p. 260.
11. *Proceedings of the Twenty-Eighth General Conference, Church of the United Brethren in Christ* (Dayton, Ohio: Otterbein Press, 1921), p. 435.
12. Ibid., p. 436.
13. Personal correspondence from Malcom M. Clippinger to the author (January 3, 1973).
14. Personal correspondence from Dr. John A. Clippinger to the author (January 3, 1973).
15. *Proceedings of the Second General Conference, The Evangelical United Brethren Church* (Dayton, Ohio: Otterbein Press, 1950), pp. 116, 117.
16. Personal correspondence from Dr. John A. Clippinger to the author (January 3, 1973).
17. *Telescope-Messenger* (Harrisburg, Pennsylvania: July 2, 1955), p. 14.
18. *Telescope-Messenger* (August 16, 1958), p. 6.

BISHOP JOHN S. STAMM

2

Statesman-Like Leadership

With the insight of a statesman, Bishop John S. Stamm set forth the task of the church in these words: "It is the task of the church to teach, but the church is more than a school. It is the task of the church to evangelize, but the church is more than a recruiting agency. It is the task of the church to minister to the needy, but the church is more than a benevolent institution. It is the task of the church to promote goodwill, but the church is more than a good-fellowship group. It is the task of the church to create social idealism, but the church is more than a social agency. It is the task of the church to combat evil and establish the good, but the church is more than a reform movement. . . the church is the body of Christ. She is the embodiment of his life, the expression of his mind and the agency for the realization of his purpose . . . Her task includes service, but also character. The church must do, but primarily she must be. . . . There is great need that the church rediscover her task, but also rediscover her true character."[1]

He gave the communion service at the 1946 Uniting Conference, in which he said: "The basic affirmation of the gospel is that 'Christ died for our sins according to the Scripture.' This is the source of Christian experience, the foundation of the Christian faith, and the distinctiveness of the Christian message. Without this there is no gospel of redemption."[2]

These brief excerpts illustrate the clarity of thought and expression so characteristic of Bishop Stamm's preaching. A former student described him as "a careful thinker and a great scholar . . . very slow, thoughtful and convincing in the classroom as well as in the pulpit."[3]

A close associate said "he was a scholarly bishop, yet he was not given to academic pomp and pretense. His messages were understandable to all thoughtful listeners, and laymen as well as ministers listened eagerly."[4]

John Samuel Stamm was born on Sunday morning, March 23, 1878, and to his parents, Hanz and Mary Stamm, this was an indication that God had a special work for him. They were devout Christians and members of the Evangelical Church in Alida, Kansas, which they had helped organize seven years earlier.

John was so disturbed by a sermon he heard one Sunday morning when ten years of age that he went to a hillside after church to pray. "I prayed because I had a very keen sense of the need of the saving grace of God in Christ. Suddenly, as I was praying there came to me a sense of peace, release and trust . . . a new joy filled my life . . . . I came into an assurance that I was a Christian . . . because I had come into personal saving relationship with God."[5]

A few Sundays later, his pastor remarked that he was growing old and would soon need to lay down his work. He asked, "Who will take my place?" As Bishop Stamm recalled that Sunday morning later, he wrote: "Instinctively, I said, 'I will.' Whether I whispered this reply audibly or only in the inner sanctuary of my soul, I do not remember. One thing I did know, and still know, is that I did make the response . . . . The shock of the experience gradually died out, but the fact that I had made the response lingered with me."[6]

Sitting with several other teenage boys one night when the preacher gave the invitation to come to the altar, John turned to his associates and said: "If I go, will you go?" They assured him they would. He said: "Then we filed down the center aisle to the altar. That night I found Jesus Christ as my personal Savior. It was an experience of great joy and meaning and still is today."[7]

John was eighteen at the time and always considered this a turning point in his life. "I now made a complete turnabout in life," he said. "Instead of doubting God, I now loved him . . . I now sought to serve Christ and the church . . . things of the spirit had new interest and challenge for me . . . the call of the Christian ministry came to me with clear and convincing urgency."[8]

He had completed less than five grades of public school when he turned twenty. That fall he sold his horse and other personal possessions to obtain enough money to purchase a train ticket to Naperville, Illinois,[9] where the Evangelical Church maintained a college and seminary. When he arrived, he applied for study in the seminary. "After a brief interview, I was informed that I did not qualify for seminary work. . . . At that time there were others who were as belated in their education as was I, and the college arranged for sub-academy courses. This opened the way for me to begin my preparation for the ministry."[10]

Twelve years later, he had completed his college work and was graduated from the seminary. In 1927, the seminary honored him with a Doctor of Divinity degree. He received a Doctor of Laws degree from Albright College in 1936, a Doctor of Humane Letters from North Central College in 1949 and Doctor of Sacred Theology from Dickinson College in 1951.

Bishop Stamm gave credit to a school teacher at Shelly Mission in Missouri, his first assignment, for making him aware of the need to preach with clarity. This teacher arose at the close of a service and said: " 'you preachers always tell us to have faith. Why don't you tell us what faith is?' . . . This criticism," he said, "led me to study more carefully the teaching content of my sermons. . . . What is the worth of words if they have no meaning? Preaching is exhortation and admonition, but basically it must be instructive." [11]

In 1901, he was appointed to the Glasgow Evangelical Mission in Missouri. "When I met the class leader at the railroad station, he greeted me rather formally, then said, 'I had better tell you right away, we do not want you.' He said they had requested the conference not to send an unmarried man to this mission. . . . I said that I was sorry they felt that way, and I was sorry that I was sent to the church. I added, however, that I had been assigned for the year and would remain." [12]

While serving here, he became acquainted with Priscilla Marie Wahl, who taught in the primary department of the Sunday school and was elected superintendent when only nineteen. On March 19, 1912, John and Priscilla Wahl were married while he was serving as pastor of Manhattan Evangelical Church. A short time later he was appointed to Oak Park Village. Even though his salary and housing allowance was very small, they rented a house large enough to provide a study, and he established study hours from 7:30 till noon every day, a practice he consistently followed as a pastor.

Two nights before Christmas in 1918, Bishop Spreng informed Pastor Stamm by telephone that he had been elected to teach systematic theology in the seminary. He remained at the seminary until elected bishop in 1926 and assigned to Kansas City. His theological scholarship was recognized in his service as a consultant editor of the *Revised Standard Version of the Bible* and of *The Interpreters Bible*.

19

During his first eight years as bishop of the Evangelical Church, he also served as the general secretary of evangelism. Following his episcopal assignment to Harrisburg, Pennsylvania, in 1934, he served as president of The School of Theology at Reading until 1941.

He gave statesman-like leadership to the Pennsylvania Council of Churches (1945-49) and to the Federal Council of Churches (1948-50) while serving as president of those organizations. He was a member of the 1948 organizational Assembly of the World Council of Churches and served on its Central Committee until 1954.

Evangelism was always a chief concern of the bishop. He defined evangelism as "an attitude which finds expression in an unceasing, cooperative effort on the part of man and God to bring men into vital personal relationship with God through faith in Jesus Christ, his Son, which is to result in a definite experience of personal salvation and a progressive building of Christlike character, bringing man into complete harmony with the will of God in all phases of life."[13]

When Bishop Stamm requested retirement at the 1950 General Conference, he said: "Through the goodness of God, I have been able to serve in the Christian ministry for more than fifty-one and a half years . . . . From the hour when I yielded to God in response to the call to the Christian ministry to this very day, I have been under a commanding sense of stewardship which impelled me to make this ministry central in my thought and life: to give Christ the preeminence in all things, and to give myself wholly to this work . . . . I can honestly say, I was not disobedient to the heavenly vision."

Speaking of his wife, he said, "Her comradeship with me in the service of the Christian ministry has been and continues to be a source of inspiration and strength to me. Whatever achievements mark these years, a large part of the credit belongs to Mrs. Stamm."

He closed his farewell address by saying, "I am not tired of the Christian ministry. . . . The years that lie ahead are in the hands of God. . . . Officially I will stand on the sidelines, but I shall cheer for our leaders. I shall do more. I shall pray."[14]

Bishop and Mrs. Stamm continued to live in Harrisburg for another four years, keeping busy responding to calls for their services. On August 31, 1954, they moved back to Kansas City, Missouri, where he first served as bishop.[15]

On Sunday morning, February 12, 1956, Bishop Stamm preached at Trinity Evangelical United Brethren Church, which he had dedicated on that same date in 1931. Five days later he was injured in a fall at his home. The illness that followed resulted in his death on March 5.[16] Funeral services were conducted from the church and burial was in Mt. Moriah Cemetery in Kansas City, Missouri.

In 1960, personal contributions from friends of the bishop endowed a council room in the Inter-Church Center Building in New York City to honor him for his many contributions in ecumenical relationships.[17]

Those who knew the bishop could agree with one of his pastors who said: "I found him to be in every sense of the word a gentleman and a scholar ... an able and dedicated churchman."[18]

Mrs. Stamm died on December 19, 1965, after a prolonged illness. Bishop Paul W. Milhouse conducted funeral services from Trinity Church on December 22. Her body was interred beside the body of Bishop Stamm.

NOTES

1. *Proceedings of the Thirty-Second General Conference of the Evangelical Church* (1938), pp. 101, 102.
2. *Proceedings of the First General Conference of the Evangelical United Brethren Church* (Dayton, Ohio: Otterbein Press, 1947), p. 70.
3. Personal correspondence from Harley E. Hiller to the author (October 18, 1972).
4. Personal correspondence from Joe Willard Krecker to the author (June 20, 1972).
5. John S. Stamm, "From Farm Boy to Bishop," *Builders,* Vol. 62 (February 26, 1955), p. 6.
6. Ibid, p. 7.
7. Ibid (February 19, 1955), p. 14.
8. Ibid (February 26, 1955), p. 7.
9. C. R. Findley, *Life Sketch of Bishop Stamm,* read at the bishop's funeral.
10. John S. Stamm, "From Farm Boy to Bishop," *Builders,* Vol. 62 (March 5, 1955), p. 4.
11. Ibid (March 12, 1955), p. 14.
12. Ibid (March 19, 1955), p. 4.
13. John S. Stamm, *Evangelism and Christian Experience* (Harrisburg, Pennsylvania: Evangelical Press, 1930), p. 23.
14. John S. Stamm, "Request for Superannuated Relationship," in *Official Proceedings*

of the Thirty-Seventh General Conference of The Evangelical United Brethren Church (Dayton, Ohio: Otterbein Press, 1950), pp. 118, 119.

15. *Telescope-Messenger* (Harrisburg, Pennsylvania: September 4, 1954), p. 11.
16. C. R. Findley, *Life Sketch of Bishop Stamm,* read at the funeral of Bishop Stamm.
17. *Telescope-Messenger* (November 14, 1959).
18. Personal correspondence from H. H. Vogel to the author (October 2, 1972).

BISHOP IRA D. WARNER

3

He Dreamed Great Dreams

"He came to the west at a time when the spirit of work in our church was at a low ebb . . . a man who dreamed great dreams and then used his life to make those dreams come true." This is the way Conference Superintendent O. E. Schafer summarized Bishop Warner's 29 years of episcopal leadership.[1]

Another wrote: "In that memorable year of 1929, Ira D. Warner, a comparatively young man of 43, was elected to the bishopric and assigned to the Pacific Area . . . a leader . . . who saw the need for enlarging the horizon of the church in this state."[2] Bishop Warner was referred to as a "five-star general" of the church by his successor, Bishop W. Maynard Sparks.[3]

Ira David Warner, whose parents were Albert and Sarah Waitman Warner, was born September 14, 1886.[4] After completing elementary school in his home community, Clayton, Ohio, he went to high school in Brookville, where he won debate and oratory contests, and silver and gold medal awards in music. Following a late Saturday night glee club rehearsal, he accepted an invitation to spend the night at his teacher's home in Brookville and attend the Brookville United Brethren Church.

When the minister gave the invitation to become a disciple of Christ, his teacher whispered to him: "Young man, you ought to be a Christian."[5] Ira responded by going to the altar. A short time later he joined the church and was elected Sunday school superintendent at eighteen.

A week-long spiritual battle ended in an attic room where Ira, alone in prayer and through a decisive surrender of himself to the lordship of Jesus Christ, finally found the inner peace and assurance which he had been seeking at the altar of the church. Out of that experience came a growing sense of call to the ministry.

Bishop Warner's mother encouraged him in his decision to enter the ministry, but his father's indifference sometimes turned to opposition in refusing the use of the carriage to go to church, which was several miles away. Father Bovey, a retired minister living in Clayton, helped Ira clarify his call to the ministry when he put his hand on his shoulder and said: "Ira, I believe God is calling you to be a minister."[6]

After graduation from Brookville high school with honors, he enrolled in Otterbein College where he became active in forensics, Bible study classes, Y.M.C.A., Life Work Recruits, Athletic Council, and played football. Shortly before graduation in June, 1911, while debating whether to continue with plans to enter the ministry or go into Y.M.C.A. work, Bishop H. H. Fout asked him to go to Chattanooga, Tennessee, to pastor the United Brethren mission.

Following his marriage to Edna Mae Landis two weeks after graduation, he took his bride to Chattanooga. Still questioning his call to the ministry, Pastor Warner became ill with nervous chills on the day he was to begin a series of evangelistic sermons. His wife told him, "You're not sick; you're scared," and insisted that he get out of bed and go to the church.[7]

The church was filled that night and seven persons responded to his altar call. This was the beginning of a life-long evangelistic ministry which was carried over into his episcopal office and expressed itself by conducting evangelistic meetings in three out of four churches in his episcopal area.

After two years in Chattanooga, he spent four years as pastor of Oak Street United Brethren Church in Dayton, Ohio, where he became known as an effective administrator and warm-hearted pastor. Then came six years of outstanding leadership at First Church in Canton. Otterbein College honored him with a Doctor of Divinity degree in 1921. Leadership in a thirteen-county Near East Relief Drive following World War I, brought him special citation from the national chairman, the Honorable William H. Taft.

He was appointed to the First United Brethren Church in Akron in 1923 where he led that congregation in completing a new building. His church arranged for him to attend the 1924 World Sunday School Convention in Glasgow and visit Europe, Egypt and Palestine. He was elected president of the Ohio Pastors' Convention while serving in Akron.

His service as bishop began in 1929 with assignment to the Pacific Area of the United Brethren Church. His report to the next General Conference reveals a passion and pattern that characterized his episcopal ministry to the end. "We have seventy-one scattered churches which I have visited from two to six times each year of this quadrennium . . . . I am glad to report that we have been able to stem the tide of decline, rekindle the spirit of fellowship and passion for souls. . . . I

25

have since last conference . . . given pastoral supervision to the Blanchard Church."[8]

Mrs. Warner died July 8, 1934. Bishop Warner told the General Conference: "I was compelled to locate my two children in Westerville where the son was in college. I have been compelled to carry on my work without the comforts and companionship of a home."[9]

Following his marriage to Ada May Visick of LaVerne, California, three years later, the couple went to England where Bishop Warner attended the 1937 Oxford Conference on Faith and Order. They also visited Mrs. Warner's relatives in Scotland. "Upon their return . . . they established their home in Pomona, California, and opened a new mission in that city. Here Mrs. Warner served as pastor for eight and a half years."[10]

Bishop Warner found time to write several books: *Christian Education in the Sunday School, Handbook on Evangelism, My Father's Business, Building the Body of Christ* and *Spiritual Priorities for Church School Leaders.*[11]

He also prepared illustrated lectures on *The Abundant Life* and *Home Mission Opportunities.*[12] York College honored him with a Doctor of Laws degree in 1942.

In 1946, Sierra Leone, West Africa, was added to Bishop Warner's episcopal assignment. He and Mrs. Warner spent five months there on their first visit, typical of the bishop's thorough search for understanding every responsibility he carried. Upon his return to the United States, he warned that "the missionary's function increasingly must be that of training leaders. He must be big enough in spirit to give up the satisfaction of having the front seat and directing the work."[13] His world outlook and understanding was recognized in his selection to represent his church at the World Council of Churches in 1954.[14]

One of Bishop Warner's most treasured possessions was his Grandfather Waitman's Bible which had a prayer written on the fly leaf. "Lord Jesus, thou hast put me in the ministry. I am but a little child; I know not how to go out or to come in; I am so unworthy of so great an honor; I shall surely fail if thou art not with me.

"If thou good Master, canst find any part in me which thy

power has not touched, then touch it. But over every part thou hast touched, there write thy name, whether brain or eye or ear, or hand, or heart, or mouth, or foot — over all, all, over all, write thy name of authority and ownership forever.

"Let me be thy faithful servant in time and thy welcome servant in eternity." [15]

To Bishop Warner "the Bible was basic to all else." [16] He once said: "The most marvelous thing recorded in the book of Acts is the change in the personalities of the disciples . . . they were to know Christ, not as a personality apart from themselves, but as an indwelling presence made possible through the work of the Holy Spirit as a new power . . . power for Christian service." [17] His life was a living demonstration of this power to serve. He set for himself a schedule that few men could physically endure.

Bishop Warner died July 1, 1964, of complications resulting from an automobile accident.[18] Burial was in Rose Hills Garden of Reflection at Whittier, California.[19] The stone marker over his grave carries the emblem of the bishop's office and the words:

Ira David Warner
Bishop
1886-1964
Preaching the gospel
was his greatest joy

NOTES

1. *Church and Home* (Harrisburg, Pennsylvania, September 1, 1964), p. 23.
2. J. Russell Davis, *From Saddlebags to Satellites* (San Diego, California: Keystone Agency, 1963), pp. 120, 123.
3. *Church and Home* (September 1, 1964), p. 23.
4. *Who Was Who in America* (Chicago: A. N. Marquis, 1968), Vol. 4 (1961-1968), p. 984.
5. Koontz and Roush, *The Bishops* (Dayton, Ohio: Otterbein Press, 1950), p. 302.
6. Ibid, p. 304.
7. Ibid, p. 307.
8. *Proceedings of the Thirty-First General Conference, Church of the United Brethren in Christ* (Dayton, Ohio: Otterbein Press, 1933), pp. 44-46.
9. *Proceedings of the Thirty-Second General Conference, Church of the United Brethren in Christ* (Dayton, Ohio: Otterbein Press, 1937), p. 41.
10. Koontz and Roush, *The Bishops*, p. 312.

27

11. *Who Was Who in America* (Chicago: A. N. Marquis, 1968), Vol. 4 (1961-1968), p. 984.
12. *Proceedings of the Thirty-Second General Conference, Church of the United Brethren in Christ,* p. 41.
13. *Telescope-Messenger* (Harrisburg, Pennsylvania, August 8, 1953), p. 11.
14. Ibid (September 11, 1954), p. 11.
15. Koontz and Roush, *The Bishops,* pp. 298-301.
16. Personal correspondence from Dr. Arthur C. Core to the author (December 18, 1972).
17. Ira David Warner, "The Power of the Holy Spirit" in *Faith in the Guidance of the Holy Spirit* (Dayton, Ohio: Otterbein Press, 1943), pp. 37-41.
18. *Kansas Conference Bulletin* (October, 1964).
19. *Church and Home* (September 7, 1964), p. 23.

BISHOP G. E. EPP

4

A Creative Administrator

"He was an exacting and creative administrator," is the way Bishop G. E. Epp was described by Harley H. Hiller, whose acquaintance and working relationship with the bishop extended over a period of 36 years. "He was known for his insistence upon correct parliamentary procedures as well as a dramatic and forceful preacher of the gospel."[1]

George Edward Epp was born in Sheboygan, Wisconsin, in 1886 and sixty-six years later returned to that city to dedicate the new Fountain Park Church building, which included a chapel-parlor named in his honor.[2]

He enrolled in Evangelical Theological Seminary in Naperville, Illinois, to prepare for the ministry and was graduated from there in 1906. While still in the seminary, he received his probationer's license to preach. He was ordained deacon in 1907 by the Wisconsin Conference. That same year he married Cora Runkel, who shared his ministry for 60 years until her death during Christmas week in 1967.[3]

When he became pastor of the Prairie du Chien Mission, stretching along the Mississippi River, he said, "I became a circuit rider." He was ordained elder in 1909 and two years later was appointed pastor of Salem Evangelical Church in Milwaukee. He was in his fifth year as pastor of First Evangelical Church in Racine when the 1919 General Conference elected him assistant executive secretary-treasurer of the Board of Missions, and on February 1, 1920, he was made the chief executive officer of that board. Cleveland, Ohio, now became home for Mrs. Epp and the three children while George Epp spent much of his time traveling over the world to supervise the mission work of his church.[4]

Elected bishop and assigned to residence in St. Paul, Minnesota, in 1930, he had responsibility for an area on both sides of the International Boundary Line extending to the Pacific Coast. In 1934, he was transferred to Naperville, Illinois, to oversee the work in Indiana, Illinois, Ohio, Wisconsin, Michigan and Ontario.[5]

Bishop Epp prepared the Episcopal Message to the 1942 General Conference. The United States was involved in World War II at the time. As he spoke of the suffering of the Evangelical Church members when Poland was invaded, he was talking about the suffering of personal friends, for he had visited many

Evangelical churches in Europe. He shared the humiliation of those churches in Lativa that had to pay rent to their conquerors for the use of their own buildings. He spoke with deep emotion when he told of District Superintendent R. Kahnmal's narrow escape from death when his home was bombed.

The optimism which was so characteristic of the bishop leaped forth in the last paragraphs of his report when he said: "These eventful, dangerous days are not the final chapter of our civilization. There will be a tomorrow."[6]

Bishop Epp gave effective leadership in bringing about the union of the Evangelical Church and the Church of the United Brethren in Christ to establish The Evangelical United Brethren Church in 1946. In the new church, he carried responsibility for general supervision of the churches in Europe in addition to his episcopal area in the United States. He became very proficient in using the German language through correspondence and repeated visits to Germany, and in his retirement years, he served the church by translating many of the German records into English. These included a biography of Jacob Albright, founder of the Evangelical Church[7] and a history of the publishing house in Stuttgart.[8]

In 1947, he and Bishop John S. Stamm went to Europe to survey the building needs of congregations which had suffered from bombings during World War II. This was the beginning of a crusade to gather money to assist the Germans in rebuilding their churches.

Bishop Epp represented his church in World Council of Churches and National Council of Churches meetings on several occasions. His enthusiasm for the church's worldwide evangelistic missionary work was rooted in his conviction that "Christianity is a missionary religion. . . . The church's chief business, as I see it," he said, "is the stimulation of mind and heart and conscience through the faithful proclamation of the gospel of Christ. . . . Her task is the cultivation of Christian attitudes and habits of life. . . . She must train in her own schools, her youth for positions of leadership and trust, lift their horizons, deepen their convictions, clarify their purpose, enrich their experiences, fire their enthusiasm and send them out to challenging tasks. . . . What the church needs at the moment is not more study or analysis of conditions. She needs

31

action. She needs power equal to her tasks. All this she can have and will have when she is willing and ready to pay the price of dedication."[9]

Bishop Epp's concept of Christian world mission was "a broad, inclusive term that covers teaching, preaching and all the varied forms of human service. . . . We do not go to the nations called non-Christian because they are the worst in the world and they alone are in need," he wrote, "we go because they are a part of the world and share with us in the same human need—the need of redemption from ourselves and from sin."[10]

In pointing out the importance of the church, he wrote: "In the New Testament there is no such thing as a Christian apart from the church. All of them belonged to the fellowship. . . . The church is a fellowship that transcends all racial, sectarian, temporal and class distinctions. . . . The business of the church is still to proclaim the gospel, to maintain the fellowship, to witness to the Saviorhood of Christ, to teach and train in worship, to meet human weaknesses and needs, to administer the cause of Christ in the world."[11]

Bishop Epp was transferred to Harrisburg, Pennsylvania, in 1950 to supervise the Evangelical United Brethren churches in Eastern Pennsylvania, Maryland and New England. Upon retirement from active service in 1958, he was given the title, Bishop Emeritus. He and Mrs. Epp moved to Riverside, Illinois, and became active in Trinity Evangelical United Brethren Church.

One who knew him well, said he was "meticulous about procedures and records. . . . I have never known another man (minister or other) who was so patient as a listener. . . . He would answer any request honestly and directly. . . . He was a man of exceptionally generous spirit, never any sign of meanness, littleness of spirit, recrimination or grudge toward those who crossed him. He could see a cherished idea or plan go down the drain, but he himself would rise to constructive service and wholesome relationships."[12]

Bishop Harold R. Heininger said of Bishop Epp at his funeral service on May 9, 1970: "His churchmanship and his Christian concerns were in his blood."[13]

NOTES

1. Personal correspondence from Dr. Harley H. Hiller (October 18, 1972).
2. *Telescope-Messenger* (Harrisburg, Pennsylvania, September 13, 1952), p. 20.
3. *Illinois Conference of the United Methodist Church, Official Record, 124th Annual Session* (1968), p. 109.
4. George E. Epp, *1968 Christmas Letter.*
5. Raymond M. Veh, *Thumbnail Sketches of Evangelical Bishops* (Harrisburg, Pennsylvania: Evangelical Press, 1939), p. 26.
6. *Proceedings of the Thirty-Third Session of the General Conference of the Evangelical Church* (1942), pp.153-154.
7. John N. Ness, Jr., *One-Hundred Fifty Years* (Dayton, Ohio: Otterbein Press, 1966), p. 23.
8. Ibid, pp. 224-233.
9. George Edward Epp, "Facing the New Quadrennium," *Telescope-Messenger,* Vol. 117 (January 27, 1951), p. 17.
10. George Edward Epp, "Good News for the World," in *Christ Calls to World-Wide Witnessing* (Dayton, Ohio: Otterbein Press, 1954), pp. 19, 21.
11. George Edward Epp, "The Great Fellowship," in *The Resources of the Church* (Dayton, Ohio: Otterbein Press, 1956), pp. 49, 50.
12. Personal correspondence from Joe Willard Krecker to the author (May 23, 1973).
13. Harold R. Heininger, "Memorial Message Honoring Bishop George Edward Epp." (May 9, 1970).

BISHOP E. W. PRAETORIUS

5

He Knew the Book

When Elmer Wesley Praetorius received his license to preach in 1904[1] at age 22, he went home and wrote on the fly leaf of his Bible: "I have but one passion for my ministry and that is to know this book and to interpret it to others."[2]

He never waivered from this goal. He had begun the study of Greek in high school and when he enrolled in Union Biblical Institute (now Evangelical Theological Seminary) in 1905, he selected the Greek-Hebrew course in order to study the Scriptures in their original languages.[3]

He became known as a Bible scholar, a man who "knew The Book." Ministers in Illinois who served under his episcopal leadership expressed what others had experienced when they stated in a formal resolution: "Whereas, he has stirred us to Christian growth and stimulated us to a renewed interest in studying the Holy Scriptures as he led us in devotional periods, be it Resolved, that we follow his teaching and example and become ourselves more devoted to Christ and the Book of Books."[4]

Elmer Wesley Praetorius was born in Dayton, Ohio, October 1, 1882,[5] the eighth child of a German immigrant couple who had been "led into a vital experience of saving grace through the preaching of John Seybert, bishop in the Evangelical Church." He was carried into the church in his mother's arms and "dedicated to God in holy baptism . . . and if God willed it, to the Christian ministry."[6]

Elmer and Julia Henrietta, daughter of the Reverend Frederick and Henrietta Schweitzer, were married June 19, 1907.[7] They went to Louisville, Kentucky, where Elmer served as pastor of the Trinity Evangelical Church and led the congregation in erecting a new building. He was ordained deacon in 1908 and two years later an elder.[8]

Following a pastorate at Kent Avenue Church in Terre Haute, Indiana, he was appointed to the First Evangelical Church in Elkhart, at that time the largest congregation in the Evangelical Church.[9] In 1919, he was elected general secretary of Christian education which included responsibility for leadership in young people's work.[10]

His high regard for the Scriptures is reflected in his appeal to young people to "engage in devotional, practical and literary Bible study, paying special attention to (1) the atmosphere in which they study, (2) the record of their daily meditations, (3) memorizing the Scriptures, and (4) sharing the values of their reading and study."[11]

In a booklet called *Seasons of the Soul,* he called attention to special opportunities for reaching children and youth with the gospel message at certain ages of development and emphasized the advantages of recruiting them for Christ at an early age. The manuscript was based upon an extensive survey which he made, first in 1920 and at later intervals to keep his information up-to-date and factual.

He insisted that "the needs of the pupil are basic and must determine the policy and program" of the Sunday school. "A school justifies its existence only if something vital happens in the lives of the pupils. . . . The purpose of the church school is to lead its pupils into a personal experiential knowledge of, and a saved relationship with Jesus Christ and into vital membership in His church . . . to help its pupils achieve the life abundant, develop a well-rounded Christian character and christianize all of their life's relationships, and prepare them for effective Christian service."[12]

The Handbook of Religion for Youth was written by Secretary Praetorius to be used by pastors in catechetical study classes.[13] His work in the field of Christian education was recognized by Evangelical Theological Seminary with an honorary Doctor of Divinity degree in 1928.[14]

E. W. Praetorius was elected bishop in 1934 and assigned to residence in St. Paul, Minnesota, where he served for 20 years.[15] In speaking of his area, he said that it "is a large area, not only in distances, problems and challenges, but it is great also in opportunities, people and congregations. It is a privilege to preach the gospel and serve the church in this area."[16]

While many church executives find themselves so occupied with administrative details that they neglect Bible study, Bishop Praetorius never lost his passion for interpreting the Scriptures and held high standards before all who taught in the church school. He wrote: "The Christian teacher must be as sound in the faith as the teacher of science must be sound in his theories and correct in his formulas. . . . What bones are to the human body, basic doctrines are to the spiritual structure of a Christian life. Without these, there is no shape or form, no ability to stand erect or to act or proceed. Sound biblical theology is essential to Christian teaching.[17]

The bishop believed that "fellowship is basic to the Christian life. . . . Christian fellowship is inherent in the idea of the Kingdom of God."[18] "This fellowship in the church emerges out of fellowship with God experienced through Jesus Christ. . . . No heathen seeks fellowship with his god. He wants his god to leave him alone. He will pay any price or make any sacrifice to have his god leave him alone."[19]

Bishop Praetorius believed in the future of the church. He wrote: "Jesus declared that the fellowship he is constructing will never become a matter of mere history, but that it will ever be a vital organism, repelling every deadly onslaught, resisting the decay of time, and perpetuating itself into all eternity. . . . The church of Jesus Christ will not go under; it will go on. . . . Victory is written on her banners!"[20]

In requesting retirement at the 1954 General Conference, he spoke in deep appreciation of his church. "It was at her altar . . . that I bowed my stubborn will and knee, and found Christ precious as my personal Savior. It was in the membership and organization of the Evangelical United Brethren Church that I found a place of service and an opportunity for growth, and it was through her ministry and the prayers of her people that I heard and answered the call to preach. . . .

"It was the General Conference . . . that elected me quadrennially, four times to the high office of general secretary of Christian education, and then five times to the highest office in her gift, to the office of bishop, making in all 35 years in general office and service in the church. It was in the fellowship of the Evangelical United Brethren Church that I found my life companion who has stood nobly and mostly silently by my side these 47½ years to encourage me, guide me and help me succeed in the ministry. It was in the Evangelical United Brethren Church that we have reared our children and it is to her ministry that we have given our only son."[21]

After retirement, "he busied himself with daily Bible study, reading other books, some writing, repairing of toys for grandchildren and neighbors (a hobby was woodworking) and photography, one of his lifetime, creative sidelines."[22]

He continued in reasonably good health until the middle of

December, 1965. He died at his home on February 2, 1966, while sitting in his favorite chair, waiting for the doctor to arrange for an ambulance to take him to the hospital. Funeral services were held two days later in Calvary Evangelical United Brethren Church, St. Paul, with Bishop R. H. Mueller and Bishop H. R. Heininger speaking at the services.

Bishop Praetorius was known as "a quiet, kindly man with a keen sense of humor and a devout love of Christ and the church . . . one of the great preachers of the church . . ."[23]

Mrs. Praetorius died five years later on June 18, 1971. Dr. Russell Praetorius, the son, wrote this tribute: "Though shy and retiring by nature, she was a devoted, loving mother and parsonage wife with her husband's ministry her consuming passion. To my knowledge she never wrote a book, held an office, chaired a meeting, gave a talk, sang a solo, marched in a demonstration, or demanded her rights. But she did know God on a personal basis, was versed in Holy Scriptures, was expert in prayer, and effective in relating scores of persons, many of whom were immigrant Hungarian women, to Jesus Christ as Savior. . . . She was a real Christian lady, she was my mother, and still is."[24]

The bodies of Bishop and Mrs. Praetorius lie side by side in Sunset Memorial Park in Minneapolis.

NOTES

1. S. H. Baumgartner, *Indiana Conference History* (Cleveland, Ohio: Evangelical Publishing House, 1915), Vol. I, p. 384.
2. *Official Proceedings of the Thirty-Eighth Session of the General Conference of the Evangelical United Brethren Church* (Dayton, Ohio: Otterbein Press, 1954), p. 124.
3. Raymond M. Veh, *Thumbnail Sketches of Evangelical Bishops* (Harrisburg, Pennsylvania: Evangelical Publishing House, 1939), p. 27.
4. *Official Proceedings of the 109th Session of the Illinois Conference (EV) of the Evangelical United Brethren Church* (1953), p. 124.
5. S. H. Baumgartner, *Indiana Conference History*, p. 96.
6. E. W. Praetorius, "An Appreciation," *Official Proceedings of the Thirty-Eighth Session of the General Conference of the Evangelical United Brethren Church* (Harrisburg, Pennsylvania: Evangelical Press, 1954), p. 123.
7. Obituary read at funeral of Mrs. E. W. Praetorius.
8. S. H. Baumgartner, *Indiana Conference History*, Vol. I, pp. 392, 393.
9. Raymond M. Veh, *Thumbnail Sketches of Evangelical Bishops*, p. 27.
10. Raymond M. Albright, *A History of the Evangelical Church* (Harrisburg, Pennsylvania: Evangelical Press, 1956), p. 347.
11. Ibid, p. 357.

12. E. W. Praetorius, *Seasons of the Soul* (Dayton, Ohio: Reprint by Board of Christian Education and Board of Evangelism, The Evangelical United Brethren Church, 1947).
13. Raymond M. Albright, *A History of the Evangelical Church,* p. 394.
14. Raymond M. Veh, *Thumbnail Sketches of Evangelical Bishops,* p. 27.
15. Raymond M. Albright, *A History of the Evangelical Church,* pp. 391, 458.
16. E. W. Praetorius, "The Northwestern Area," *Telescope-Messenger,* Vol. 117 (June 2, 1951), p. 10.
17. E. W. Praetorius, "Four Questions," *Telescope-Messenger,* Vol. 47 (March 24, 1951), pp. 16, 24.
18. E. W. Praetorius, "The Value of Christian Fellowship," in *Christian Fellowship* (Dayton, Ohio: Otterbein Press, 1947), pp. 19, 20.
19. Ibid, p. 13.
20. E. W. Praetorius, "Christ's Church will Win," in *My Church Faces Union* (Dayton, Ohio: Otterbein Press, 1944), pp. 87, 91.
21. E. W. Praetorius, "An Appreciation," in *Official Proceedings of the Thirty-Eighth Session of the General Conference,* pp. 123, 124.
22. *Church and Home* (Harrisburg, Pennsylvania, April 15, 1966), p. 27.
23. Personal correspondence from Dr. L. L. Huffman to the author (January 29, 1973).
24. E. Russell Praetorius, "A Tribute to a Real Christian Lady," in Order of Worship for funeral service (June 22, 1971).

BISHOP C. H. STAUFFACHER

6

A Life-Time of Dedicated Service

When Charles Stauffacher entered the ministry, he wrote on the fly leaf of his Bible:

> I am only one, but I am one; I cannot do everything, but I can do something. What I can do, I ought to do, and what I ought to do, by the grace of God, I will do.
>
> C. H. Stauffacher[1]

What followed was a lifetime of dedicated service to his church. A minister who served under his episcopal leadership said: "He was a dedicated churchman and a forceful preacher of the word."[2] Another described him as "a hard-working, efficient executive, a man of strong convictions and great loyalty."[3]

Charles Henry Stauffacher, born in Cedar Rapids, Iowa, October 27, 1879, was the son of the Reverend John and Rose Raymer Stauffacher. After graduating from the city's public schools, he enrolled in Highland Park College and later transferred to Des Moines University where he received his Bachelor of Science degree in 1901.[4] While in college, he served as secretary of the college Y.M.C.A., president of the junior class, an officer in the athletic association and was active in the glee club.[5]

He was licensed to preach in 1901 by the United Evangelical Church and appointed to Anita, Iowa. Here he met Madge Ruth Worthing whom he married on March 23, 1905. Then followed pastorates in Belle Plaine, Waterloo, Zering and Cedar Rapids, and four years as district superintendent.

He became associate secretary of the General Missionary Society in 1921, and for the next thirteen years, his ministry was related to the mission work of his church. He was assigned to residence in Kansas City, Missouri, when elected bishop in 1934, with responsibility for churches in Iowa, Missouri, Kansas, Nebraska, Texas, Oklahoma, and before the Union of the Evangelical and United Brethren churches, he also supervised the churches in Colorado and California.[6] He was sent to the Orient in 1937 to organize the China Conference and visit the church's work in Japan and Hong Kong. He visited the Pacific Area again in 1946 and 1954.[7]

As the Evangelical Church and the United Brethren Church moved toward union, Bishop Stauffacher expressed his con-

cern for the rituals to be "beautiful, dignified and worshipful
. . . gather up out of the rich literature of worship that which
has been most helpful . . . of such a character that ministers will
be expected to use them, and people will be edified by them." [8]

When the churches united in 1946, the bishop was assigned
responsibility for selecting a committee to combine and rewrite
the rituals of the churches. Eight years of work by this committee under his leadership produced new rituals that combined
the richness and beauty of historical language and form with an
up-to-date relevance that made them immediately popular with
the church. A book entitled, *Christian Worship in Symbol and
Ritual* was written by Paul W. Milhouse under the guidance of
the committee to provide pastors with historical background,
interpretation and guidance for using the new rituals.

Bishop Stauffacher's ability to clearly comprehend and state
religious values is evident in this statement: "The Christian
religion is partly an inheritance and partly an experience. The
values of an inheritance must be carefully considered before
any part thereof is discarded or permanently retained. The
values of an experience must be analyzed to be sure that they
rest on a secure basis and not on a transitory emotional state.
Our Christian religion must be studied so that both our inheritance and our experience will provide a sound basis for our
religious beliefs and practices." [9]

Bishop Stauffacher called stewardship the "Christian
philosophy of life. It is applied Christianity. It is a practical way
of living. . . . Christian stewardship is related to all a Christian is
and has and does; to the whole of life and every aspect of life
. . . a recognition of God's ownership of all things both material
and spiritual. . . . Man's ownership of material things is more
apparent than real. . . It has been said that Christianity has not
been tried and found wanting, but it was found difficult and
not tried." [10]

Dr. Stanley B. Williams worked with Bishop Stauffacher in
uniting former Evangelical and United Brethren conferences.
"In all of these negotiations," he wrote, "the wisdom, guidance,
knowledge and kindly direction of Bishop Stauffacher cannot
be overestimated. . . . It was the statesmanlike leadership of
Bishop Stauffacher that carried this area through the most
difficult and often vexatious negotiations concerning the union

of York College with Westmar. . . . He was an able, decisive speaker, and an almost perfect administrator. . . . He was as true a friend as I ever had."[11]

Bishop Stauffacher came to the 1954 General Conference in Milwaukee with the request for retirement. He said: "It has been a great honor to have been a minister of the gospel in the Evangelical United Brethren Church. I have had many offers to serve elsewhere, but this church is my love. . . . I have been happy in the work. . . . I have loved my work. It has been the chief passion of my life. I have carried no side lines. I have engaged in no hobbies, not even theological. I have taken few vacations and none since I have been in general work. I have given my full time to the ministry. . . . My greatest desire has been to be a good minister of Jesus Christ. I have demanded more of myself than mere faithfulness. I have insisted on a fair degree of effectiveness. I have not been satisfied to go through the motions of the ministry. . . .

"In all these offices and honors that have been accorded me, I have nothing to boast about. I am what I am by the grace of God. I owe much to my Christian parents. They were converted early in life, my father when eleven years old . . . my mother when eight years old. . . . They established their home on Christian principles. . . .

"I owe a great debt to my family, my wife—companion of fifty years—my three sons and a daughter who have always been a help and inspiration. If I deserve any honor or credit for what I am or what I have done, the greater share goes to them. Then, too, I have been fortunate in my friends. . . . I am grateful to you and the church you represent for your confidence, encouragement and expressions of appreciation."[12]

Following retirement, Bishop and Mrs. Stauffacher moved to a house adjoining the Western Home in Cedar Falls, Iowa.

Mrs. Stauffacher died on April 24, 1955, less than a year after the bishop's retirement. "In spite of her battle with arthritis, she produced beautifully written letters by the hundreds. She made it her practice to write two letters each year to all of our missionaries. These letters were lengthy and brought a message of cheer and encouragement to all. . . . Even though she was confined to her room for five full years at one time, everyone who called on her went away having received a blessing."[13]

Bishop Stauffacher's dedication and effectiveness as a church leader was recognized by Westmar College with the granting of a Doctor of Divinity degree in 1927 while he was still in his early ministry. North Central College honored him with a Doctor of Laws degree in 1945.[14]

Bishop Stauffacher died in Cedar Falls, Iowa, November 14, 1956, and was buried in the Linwood Cemetery beside his wife. Declining health dated back to a failure on the part of his overworked heart to function properly on December 26, 1953. A Stauffacher Memorial Fund was established as permanent endowment at Westmar College with the income to be used for scholarship aid.[15]

NOTES

1. Personal correspondence from Mrs. Clarence (Joy) Stauffacher Attig to the author (September 30, 1972).
2. Personal correspondence from Dr. H. Vogel to the author (October 2, 1972).
3. Personal correspondence from Dr. C. R. Findley to the author (July 21, 1972)
4. *Who Was Who in America* (Chicago: A. N. Marquis Company, 1960), Vol. 3 (1951-1960), p. 814.
5. Raymond M. Veh, *Thumbnail Sketches of Evangelical Bishops* (Harrisburg, Pennsylvania: Evangelical Publishing House, 1939), p. 28.
6. *Telescope-Messenger* (Harrisburg, Pennsylvania: December 15, 1956), p. 14.
7. *Kansas City Star* (November 15, 1956).
8. C. H. Stauffacher, "Differences and Likenesses," in *My Church Faces Union* (Dayton, Ohio: Otterbein Press, 1944), p. 42.
9. C. H. Stauffacher, "Christ Calls to Faithful Stewardship," *Christ Calls to Christian Growth* (Dayton, Ohio: Otterbein Press, 1953), p. 51.
10. Ibid., pp. 52-56.
11. Stanley B. Williams, *The Southwestern Area as I Have Known It* (Kansas City: Kansas Conference, Evangelical United Brethren Church, 1968), pp. 58-59.
12. Charles H. Stauffacher, "The Time Has Come," in *Proceedings of the Third General Conference of the Evangelical United Brethren Church* (Dayton, Ohio: Otterbein Press, 1954), p. 125.
13. *Telescope-Messenger* (May 21, 1955), p. 22.
14. *Who Was Who in America*, Vol. 3, p. 814.
15. *Kansas Conference Bulletin* (Topeka: December, 1959).

BISHOP V. O. WEIDLER

7

A Kind and Gracious Man

Many remember Bishop V. O. Weidler "as a very kindly person and very gracious in his attitude toward everyone in all situations. He exemplified this at his annual conferences where he was so courteous and kind." [1]

One who worked closely with him for many years said: "He was a man of broad culture, striking personality, and very great kindness . . . was always liked by the ministers of his area, a fact that was not at all strange considering he was such a kind and gracious personality." [2]

Victor Otterbein Weidler was born in the United Brethren Church parsonage at Highspire, Pennsylvania, January 27, 1887. His parents, the Reverend Zur Abner and Lydia Alice Weidler[3] named their son after Philip William Otterbein, founder and first bishop of the Church of the United Brethren in Christ.

This pride in the United Brethren Church was evident when the Reverend Z. A. Weidler stood before the 1945 General Conference and told of a visit he had one time with a lady who had been confirmed by Bishop Otterbein in his church in Baltimore. He said, "So there is only one link between my life and that of the founder of the Church of the United Brethren in Christ." [4]

The bishop's father was known as a Hebrew scholar. He "read his English Bible and Hebrew Bible simultaneously every day until his death" in 1949 at ninety years of age.[5] He quoted the first Psalm in Hebrew to the 1945 General Conference when he was eighty-six years old.[6]

Both of the bishop's grandfathers were ministers in the United Brethren Church. Joshua Harper held only a local preacher's license, but he organized several churches in Maryland and Virginia.[7] His grandfather Isaac C. Weidler was known for his evangelistic preaching.[8]

During his early boyhood, Victor complained about changing schools because of changes in his father's assignments, but he always looked forward to summertime when his mother would take the children to the family cottage at Mt. Gretna Park assembly grounds as soon as the public schools closed in the spring. They remained there until time for school to open in the fall. His father would come whenever he could get away from his church. Bishop Weidler often spoke of the impact of these summer experiences upon his life.[9]

He was converted under his father's preaching at Lykens, Pennsylvania. After graduation from Lykens high school, he enrolled in Lebanon Valley College. Here he sang in the glee club and pursued his interest in music. He received the Bachelor of Arts degree in 1910 and did graduate work at Columbia University the following summer in preparation for a teaching career. While teaching in Waynesboro high school, he came to the conviction that he ought to preach and determined to continue teaching school only long enough to pay off his school debts.[10]

The Waynesboro Charge granted him a quarterly conference license to preach in 1913. At the close of the school term, he worked as an evangelistic singer. In the fall of that year, he was appointed to serve as pastor at Frewsburg, New York. During his three years here, Pastor Weidler developed a strong teacher-training program and led the congregation in a new building project. The members of an independent church at Stillwater, three miles away, were so impressed with the help received from his training classes that they asked to become a part of the Erie Annual Conference of the United Brethren Church.[11]

Victor was ordained an elder on September 3, 1916, and appointed to the Elmwood Church in Buffalo, New York. He was married to Dora Henrietta Housekeeper on his birthday, January 27, 1920, in the home of her parents in Bowling Green, Ohio. Dora, who had been reared in a United Brethren home, was a graduate of Ohio Northern University, taught at the mission schools in New Mexico and served five years as field secretary for the Women's Missionary Association.[12]

The Weidlers went to Minneapolis in 1926 where he served eight years as pastor of the local church and superintendent of the Minnesota Conference. A year after becoming executive secretary of Home Missions and Church Erection, Lebanon Valley College honored him with a Doctor of Divinity degree in recognition of his outstanding churchmanship and the effective leadership he was giving to the mission work of the church. York College honored him with a Doctor of Laws degree in 1942.

The 1937 General Conference delegates elected Doctor

Weidler bishop on mail ballot to fill the vacancy created by the death of Bishop Arthur B. Stratton.[13] The Weidlers moved to Kansas City in May, 1938, where Bishop Weidler was to serve as the episcopal leader for Iowa, Nebraska, Kansas, Missouri, Oklahoma, Colorado and New Mexico conferences.[14]

He believed a bishop's "vision must be comprehensive in both time and space. He must catch the spirit of the heroic souls who established the work in pioneer days, and he must sense the present-day demands made upon the church by the denomination and by the Christian fellowship in the more ecumenical sense."[15]

When Bishop Weidler spoke at the centennial celebration in Highspire, Pennsylvania, he was presented a gavel made from the staircase of the old Highspire parsonage where he was born. This became one of his most treasured possessions.

At the 1945 General Conference, Bishop Weidler reported three special emphases in his area which reflected his goals in church administration. "They are: First, the lifting of the rural church to its rightful place of usefulness; second, the creation of a city church with an adequate program of impact upon urban life; and third, the creation of a standardized training agency for providing an adequate leadership to man these rural and urban units of Christian influence."[16]

His insight into human nature and the Christian faith is evident when he wrote: "There are many holy impulses in life's experience toward the abundant life which Jesus offers to human kind, but these promptings of the heart are met with hesitancies, postponements and rejections. . . . Jesus always assaulted the citadel of the human personality, which is the will. He rested his case not alone in the heart, nor yet in the understanding, but in the will. Here Jesus sought a verdict."[17]

Bishop Weidler was convinced that evangelism was the central task of the church. Throughout his ministry, he planned to assist some minister in at least one evangelistic meeting each year. He loved people and had a compassion to share the gospel with all he met. He would stop strangers in the hotel lobby and invite them to go to church with him. He would walk up and down the aisles of the church when giving the invitation, pleading for people to accept Christ.

When Bishop Weidler returned from a trip, he shared with

his wife many stories about the interesting people he met on the train, in railway stations, on the streets and in the meetings he attended.

Mrs. Weidler said, "he never wasted time on the road and usually could be found reading a good book, jotting down sermon ideas that came to him. He loved his books, took good care of them, marked in them, but he didn't want anyone else to write in them."[18]

On his way to Kitchener, Ontario, to attend the 1950 Christian Education Convention, Bishop Weidler suffered a cerebral hemorrhage. He was taken to the hospital in Chatham, Ontario, and died three days later. Funeral services were held in Bowling Green, Ohio, on August 7 and his body was laid to rest in the cemetery there.

NOTES

1. Personal correspondence from L. L. Huffman to the author (January 29, 1973).
2. Stanley B. Williams, *The Southwestern Area as I have Known It* (Kansas City: Kansas Conference of the Evangelical United Brethren Church, 1968), pp. 55-56.
3. Koontz and Roush, *The Bishops* (Dayton, Ohio: Otterbein Press, 1950), Vol. II, p. 316.
4. *Proceedings of the Thirty-Fourth General Conference of the United Brethren Church* (Dayton, Ohio: Otterbein Press, 1945), p. 208.
5. Personal correspondence from Mrs. V. O. Weidler to the author (November 12, 1972),
6. *Proceedings of the Thirty-Fourth General Conference of the United Brethren Church*, p. 209.
7. Koontz and Roush, *The Bishops*, p. 319.
8. J. A. Angell in the *Religious Telescope* (Dayton, Ohio: May 7, 1938), pp. 8-9.
9. Personal correspondence from Mrs. V. O. Weidler to the author (November 12, 1972).
10. Ibid.
11. Ibid.
12. Koontz and Roush, *The Bishops*, p. 323.
13. Ibid, p. 328.
14. Davis, Polson, et. al, *Eighty Years in Oklahoma and Texas* (Shawnee, Oklahoma: American Printing Company, 1968), p. 199.
15. *Proceedings of the Thirty-Third General Conference of the United Brethren Church* (Dayton, Ohio: Otterbein Press, 1941), pp. 49-50.
16. *Proceedings of the Thirty-Fourth General Conference of the United Brethren Church* (Dayton, Ohio: Otterbein Press, 1945, p. 370.
17. Victor O. Weidler, "The Witness of the Holy Spirit," in *Faith in the Guidance of the Holy Spirit* (Dayton, Ohio: Otterbein Press, 1943), pp. 53, 54.
18. Personal correspondence from Mrs. V. O. Weidler to the author (November 12, 1972).

BISHOP FRED L. DENNIS

8

Patient and Gentle in Leadership

Those who sat in the assemblies and conferences over which Fred L. Dennis presided often spoke of the wise and gentle manner in which he conducted the business. A resolution of appreciation unanimously passed by one conference read: "We extend our gratitude to our bishop, Fred L. Dennis, for his patient and gentle leadership...."[1]

A district superintendent said of him: "I value above price the fellowship in the work and the wise and kindly counsel of Bishop Dennis. He is a churchman of highest rank, not only in office and name, but in spirit and understanding."[2] Another said: "He has every minister and congregation on his heart."[3]

His gentle firmness in holding to fair and correct parliamentary procedures and the relaxed manner and ease with which he presided, inspired confidence in his leadership and cooperation from those with whom he worked.

Fred Lewis Dennis was born in a log cabin, November 21, 1890, two miles southwest of Gwynneville, Indiana, the youngest of three children born to John William and Sarah Young Dennis. His mother died when Fred was five years old, and the family moved into the village of Gwynneville. The older daughter, who was thirteen at the time, became housekeeper for the family and mother to her younger sister and brother. When John Dennis married again nine years later, Fred became deeply impressed with the Christian faith and devotion of his stepmother. After breakfast each morning, she would go to some quiet corner to read her Bible. Dated records on blank pages of her Bible indicate that she read the Old Testament eleven times and the New Testament thirteen.[4]

His stepmother's faith became Fred's personal faith one night as he and a cousin knelt beside the davenport in his cousin's home. The boys were alone. The rest of the family had gone to church. Their conversation turned to religion. "Fred," said his cousin, "isn't this the time that you ought to give your life to Christ?"

Fred replied, "No, I'm not under conviction." He said later, "I had heard people say they could not eat or sleep for weeks because of their sins. Up to that time I had lost neither appetite nor sleep because of my sins."

His cousin continued to press his point by saying, "But you know that you are sinner, don't you?"

51

"Oh, yes," replied Fred, "anyone who is not a Christian must be a sinner."

"Then if you know that you are a sinner, you know that you need a Savior."

That was a new thought to Fred. The two young men knelt beside the davenport to pray together and, said Bishop Dennis, "I realized peace of soul. . . ." The two hurried to the church where services had begun, and he gave witness to his faith in Christ. His pastor mentioned the gospel ministry to him, but he had no convictions of duty that led in that direction at that time.[5]

Following graduation from Rushville high school in 1908 and two years of teaching in a township school, he enrolled at Indiana Central College. While listening to a baccalaureate speaker, he was strongly moved toward the ministry. "For the following week I was in great distress," he said, "desiring only to be certain that the call was from God. In this frame of mind I approached a table that was covered with a miscellaneous assortment of books, evidently the remains of the library of a deceased minister. I lifted a book from the pile and opened it casually. Across the top of the page I read the title of the chapter: 'What Constitutes a Call to the Ministry.' I read the address. . . . It was the answer to my need. In the decision that followed I found a peace that was comparable to that of my conversion experience."[6]

Fred Dennis was licensed to preach in August, 1910, and a year later was admitted to probationary membership in the White River Conference. He and Anna Maude Sullivan were married on December 20, 1911. A month later he was called out of his college German class and offered the pulpits of Greenwood Circuit. He accepted the assignment with such enthusiasm that he did not return to class but immediately began making preparations to move to the charge. He preached his first sermon from Galatians 6:14: "God forbid that I should glory, save in the cross of our Lord Jesus Christ."[7] The dedication reflected in this text characterized his forty-seven years of service in the ministry.

Following ordination in his senior year of college, he was appointed pastor of the college church. After graduation from Indiana Central College in 1916, he enrolled in Bonebrake (now United) Theological Seminary. He became pastor of Euclid Avenue United Brethren Church in Dayton, Ohio, following graduation from seminary, and seven years later was elected superintendent of the Miami Conference. Indiana Central College awarded him an honorary Doctor of Divinity degree in 1927.

After serving three years as superintendent, he spent twelve years as pastor of First United Brethren Church in Dayton, Ohio. When elected bishop in 1941, he was assigned to Indianapolis, Indiana, with responsibility for conferences in Indiana, Illinois, Wisconsin, Michigan and Minnesota. Otterbein College honored him with a Doctor of Laws degree in 1947.[8]

"He was known for his courage as a churchman to challenge the wrong and to give utmost support to the righteousness that is a part of the Gospel."[9] This courage is evident when he wrote: "While we tolerantly concede the right of others to their individual views, we vehemently declare anew our belief in the deity of our Lord and Savior Jesus Christ . . . . Our age is heir to the backwash of low morals . . . . Silly sentimentality upon the part of thousands gave organized forces of vice and dissipation the very opportunity they desired . . . . We are in sore need of a revival of intolerance toward sin, regardless of its form of expression."[10]

The bishop's personal devotional practice was adapted from that of George Mueller of Bristol who spent the first two hours each morning in Bible reading and prayer. He said: "As I read prayerfully, I sought to be alert to interpretations of Truth that the Spirit would bring to me out of the lesson. These suggestions were recorded in my composition book for later consideration. I began with Philippians. . . . My personal devotional commentary on Philippians remains a valued part of my personal library. . . . Daily communion with God through the word will fortify the spirit against the subtle temptation to inertia, and will on the other hand assure increased sensitivity to the will of God."[11]

His clear insight into the values and responsibilities of Christian fellowship are evident in this statement: "'Blest be the tie that binds our hearts in Christian love' is more than a line in a well-known hymn; it is the revelation of a basic kinship which exists among those who have experienced the new birth in which 'old things pass away and all things become new.' . . . The basis of fellowship in a local church is a common faith in Jesus Christ as the Son of God. This faith involves acceptance of him as Savior and Lord." [12]

He insisted that "legitimate business must be managed with due regard to the 'brotherhood.' A proper recognition of God as owner, to whom a full and accurate accounting is to be made daily, lifts the daily routine to a level of partnership with the Eternal. Stewardship becomes a privilege rather than an obligation." [13]

Bishop Dennis described sin as "the basic disturbance in our lives" and "under the inspiration of the faithful preaching of the word, supported by godly examples of devout Christians about us, we come under the conviction of sin . . ." He believed our hope is in "confessions that recognize personal inability to cope with sin that lead to humble acceptance of union with God through Jesus Christ," but such "confessions are futile unless they are followed with appropriate attitudes and actions representative of a new life." [14]

Bishop Dennis died January 28, 1958, and his body was buried in Memorial Park Cemetery in Dayton, Ohio. Bishop George E. Epp's funeral sermon summed up his life and ministry as "dedicated leadership . . . friendly, affable, courteous, amiable in response to others, sociable, mindful of others, tender in relationship, firm when necessary, forthright, deepseated in conviction." [15] Bishop J. Gordon Howard said: "The church has lost a wise administrator. The world has lost a warm-hearted, faithful and effective Christian leader." [16]

Mrs. Dennis died April 23, 1972, and was buried beside her husband. She was eighty one. Dr. Charles W. Peckham, who had long and close association with Bishop and Mrs. Dennis, said of her, "She was a faithful companion to her husband . . . never tried to compete with him for leadership . . . kind to her children, faithful to her friends and obedient to her Lord." [17]

NOTES

1. *Illinois Conference of the Church of the United Brethren in Christ, 98th Annual Session* (1944), p. 78.
2. L. L. Baughman, "Conference Superintendents Report" in *Illinois Conference of the Evangelical United Brethren Church, 102nd Annual Session* (1948), p. 39.

3. *Illinois Conference of the Evangelical United Brethren Church, 103rd Annual Session* (1949), p. 32.
4. Koontz and Roush, *The Bishops* (Dayton, Ohio: Otterbein Press, 1950), pp. 330-333.
5. Ibid, pp. 334-335.
6. Ibid, p. 336
7. Ibid, p. 338
8. *Telescope-Messenger* (Harrisburg, Pennsylvania, February 22, 1958), p. 14.
9. Personal correspondence from Dr. Arthur C. Core to the author (December 21, 1972).
10. Fred L. Dennis, "A Plea for Intolerance," *Telescope-Messenger,* Vol. 118 (March 22, 1952), p. 16.
11. Fred L. Dennis, "The Living Word," *Telescope Messenger,* Vol. 119 (January 28, 1953), p. 15.
12. Fred L. Dennis, "Forward Through Local Church Fellowship" *Christian Fellowship* (Dayton, Ohio: Otterbein Press, 1947), pp. 64, 67.
13. Ibid, p. 63
14. Fred L. Dennis, "Human Personality," in *The Resources of the Church* (Dayton, Ohio: Otterbein Press, 1956), pp. 70, 71, 78.
15. *Telescope-Messenger* (February 28, 1958), p. 14.
16. Ibid.
17. Personal correspondence from Dr. Charles W. Peckham to the author (March 20, 1973).

BISHOP J. BALMER SHOWERS

9

Converted on a Country Road

"My conversion at the age of twelve was something sure and without question in my mind," J. B. Showers told the 1954 General Conference delegates. "I know where it happened: It was on the highway. I know when it happened: It was on a Sunday afternoon in the midst of a summer day. I know the steps leading to the decision."[1]

That morning John had been one of seven boys in a Sunday school class taught by Father McComb, who had requested each boy to share his Christian faith. After some of the boys had expressed themselves, "he got to me," said John and "he said, 'What have you to say for Jesus?' I said, 'Nothing.' Then he went after me!

"Father and I went home with Mr. Emerson for dinner. . . . I couldn't eat. Finally we started home. We came to a certain place in the road. . . . I said, 'what would you say if I testified this afternoon?' He said, 'Boy, it would be the happiest day of my life.'[2] Something similar happened to that which occurred in the life of Paul on the Damascus Road . . . the light shed upon my vision on that country road leading from one worship service to another has never been dimmed."[3]

John Balmer Showers, named for the physician who attended his mother at his birth,[4] was born September 29, 1879, at Paris, Ontario, Canada, son of the Reverend Joseph and Margaret Showers.[5] His boyhood was spent in the small towns and open country of Ontario Province where his father served as pastor of United Brethren churches. He was active in Christian Endeavor, led prayer meetings, taught a Sunday school class, and while still in his "teens," served as Sunday school superintendent.[6]

He was granted a license to preach at eighteen, which he said he would refuse because he had not asked for it. The next morning was Sunday. After the sermon, the district superintendent walked over to the choir and taking John by the arm, led him to a table where he had placed his license and said to the congregation: "He's like my own son, we'll have to whip him in the traces, but he'll pull after we get him in."[7]

Ontario Conference received him into membership on probation October 13, 1899. When his father became ill in November of that year, he withdrew from Galt Collegiate Institute to pastor his father's church in Sheffield. On February 1,

1900, he began serving as pastor in Deckard, Pennsylvania.

Referring to his ordination in 1902, he said, "there came something new and elevating, something that has never been lost from my life in that hour when Bishop J. S. Mills . . . placed his hands upon my head and set me apart in Holy Orders. From that hour until this, there has never been a wavering in the conviction of my call, nor regret from the way I had been led, nor my final affirmation of response."[8]

He transferred his college credits to Lebanon Valley College and after completing his requirements for graduation, enrolled in Bonebrake (now United) Theological Seminary. Upon graduation in 1910, he was invited to teach in the field of New Testament Interpretation. To better prepare himself for this, he studied at the University of Chicago and the University of Berlin. Lebanon Valley College honored him with a Doctor of Divinity degree in 1919 and Indiana Central College gave him a Doctor of Laws degree in 1947.[9]

On April 11, 1911, he married Justina Lorenz, a graduate of Bryn Mawr College. Her father, Dr. E. S. Lorenz, was widely known as president of Lebanon Valley College and later as music publisher and editor of the United Brethren Church Hymnal. Justina's grandfather, Edward Lorenz, served as superintendent of United Brethren churches in Germany and editor of the *Botschafter.* Her mother was Florence Kumler, the granddaughter of Bishop Henry Kumler, Jr., and the great granddaughter of Bishop Henry Kumler, Sr.[10]

While serving on the seminary faculty, Doctor Showers introduced seminars and revisions in curriculum, and spent a year in study and research in Palestine, Egypt, Syria and Asia Minor. After seventeen years with the seminary, he was elected associate editor of *The Religious Telescope,* the official weekly paper of the United Brethren Church.

In 1931, Doctor Showers was asked to take charge of the finances of the United Brethren Publishing House which faced serious financial difficulties and a debt of approximately two million dollars. Dayton bankers had agreed to make further loans only on this condition. They had seen Doctor Showers guide the Dayton Chautauqua Association through its financial difficulties following the disastrous flood of 1913 and believed he could save the Publishing House.

By 1945, all indebtedness had been paid and the Publishing House was operating at a profit. "That experience was a test, unknown to others, of my physical stamina, but above that, of Christian convictions in relation to church and business," said Doctor Showers. "I found what it is to stand alone and to hear the call to flee as did Elijah; but the loyalty of my fellow-employees, the cooperation of the main creditors, and the encouragement of almost all of the church membership who understood the situation helped me maintain a courageous spirit."[11]

The 1945 General Conference elected Doctor Showers bishop to supervise the churches in Eastern United States, and in 1950, he was transferred to Indianapolis. His leadership as bishop was as distinguished as it had been in all other positions he had served. He had the reputation of "competent adminis-ter, a wise counselor and a forceful preacher of the word."[12] And he lived up to his reputation.

Bishop Showers' philosophy of leadership is revealed in one of his reports which reads in part, "God, not man is the ultimate determiner of the destinies of men and institutions . . . . Our yesterdays enter into our daily achievements or failures. . . . No man labors alone, however gifted he may be and whatever his place of leadership. The men who surround him in a vital way go into the making of his success. The unseen elements, how-ever, are stronger still. The motives that move him, the objec-tives that determine his activities and the principles of action by which he is guided play no small part in his success. But above all it is God who shapes the years of human and institutional destiny."[13]

Bishop Showers requested retirement at the 1954 General Conference. In his closing remarks at that time he said: "All that I am and all that I have, including my wife, is due to the church, the United Brethren in Christ and now the Evangelical United Brethren. Everything that has come to me goes back into the life of the family into which I was born, into the family in which I have served, and into the church which has given me an opportunity to serve. Any success that has crowned my effort is due primarily to you comrades and above all to God. I trust some years of service still await me. I feel the purpose of God for my life in official relationship has been fulfilled. I love the church and for her my tears and prayers and toils shall be given till life shall end."[14]

Death claimed Bishop Showers on September 25, 1962, just four days short of his eighty-third birthday. Funeral services were held at the Showers' home in Dayton, Ohio, on Friday, September 28, with burial in the Memorial Park Cemetery.[15]

Bishop J. Gordon Howard described Bishop Showers as "a constant and voracious reader. He loved books and had one of the largest private libraries to be found anywhere. He not only enjoyed the contents of a book, but he obtained pleasure from the feel of a well-printed and well-bound book.

"He was a man of great enthusiasm and . . . shared with Mrs. Showers a spirit of warm hospitality. While connected with the seminary, their home was always open to students. In more recent years their home became a "Mecca" for missionaries on furlough and their spacious and comfortable home in Dayton was remodelled to provide living quarters for missionary families temporarily residing in Dayton."[16]

Another who knew him well said: "He had depth of scholarship, breadth of vision, lively sense of humor, capacity for friendship, generosity of heart, graciousness of spirit, and devotion to his church. He will be remembered as a scholar, a business man and bishop, and his ministry excelled in all three of these roles."[17]

NOTES

1. *Official Proceedings of the Thirty-Eighth Session of the General Conference of the Evangelical United Brethren Church* (Dayton, Ohio: Otterbein Press, 1954), p. 127.
2. Paul C. Bailey, *A Biographical Sketch of John Balmer Showers* (A thesis in partial fulfillment of requirements for a course in Evangelical United Brethren Church history at United Theological Seminary, 1960), p. 3.
3. J. Balmer Showers, *My First Fifty Years* (Manuscript loaned by Mrs. J. B. Showers to the author), pp. 2-5.
4. Paul C. Bailey, *A Biographical Sketch of John Balmer Showers*, p. 1.
5. *Who Was Who in America* (Chicago: A. N. Marquis Company, 1968), Vol. 4 (1961-1968), p. 861.
6. Koontz and Roush, *The Bishops* (Dayton, Ohio: Otterbein Press, 1950), Vol. II p. 348.
7. *Official Proceedings of the Thirty-Eighth Session of the General Conference of the Evangelical United Brethren Church*, p. 127.
8 J. Balmer Showers, *My First Fifty Years*, p. 3.
9. *National Encyclopedia of American Biography*, p. 231.

10. Koontz and Roush, *The Bishops,* Vol. II, pp. 351-352.
11. J. Balmer Showers, *My First Fifty Years,* p. 4.
12. Paul Gibble, *History of East Pennsylvania Conference* (Dayton, Ohio: Otterbein Press, 1951), p. 475.
13. *Proceedings of the Thirty-Fourth Session of the General Conference, Church of the United Brethren in Christ* (Dayton, Ohio: Otterbein Press, 1945), p. 456.
14. J. Balmer Showers, "My Retirement" in *Proceedings of the Thirty-Eighth General Conference, The Evangelical United Brethren Church* (Dayton, Ohio: Otterbein Press, 1954), p. 129.
15. *Telescope-Messenger* (November 10, 1962), p. 12.
16. Personal correspondence from Glen E. Donelson to the author (December 19, 1972).
17. Ibid.

BISHOP D. T. GREGORY

10

A Snowstorm Changed His Life

A snowstorm that swept across the West Virginia countryside forced David Gregory and a friend to give up their plans to attend a dance. Wanting to go somewhere, they decided to attend the revival meeting at nearby Pleasant Plains United Brethren Church. That night changed his life. Here is the way he told it:

"A friend and I had planned to drive some fifteen miles with horse and buggy to attend a dance to which we had been invited. A severe snow storm began early in the afternoon, and we decided to forego the trip. A revival was on at our church. My father was in charge of the music. He directed the choir. Naturally all the family, with the one exception, had planned to be in the meeting. Then my friend and I elected to go to the meeting, having been disappointed in not being able to attend the dance.

"When my mother discovered I was going to the meeting, she elected to remain at home. Her voice lingers in my ear yet as I heard her say to my father, 'Joe, I don't believe I will go with you tonight.' When Dad expressed his concern about her being alone, she replied, 'that will be all right. Perhaps I can do more good here.'

"That night, in that revival service, God spoke to me concerning my rebellious attitude toward his call . . . my heart answered back in the affirmative and my whole life was completely changed."[1]

David Thomas Gregory was born July 16, 1889, near Martinsburg, West Virginia. His parents were Joseph T. and Sarah H. Fulk Gregory, both of whom were devout Christians and loyal members of the United Brethren Church. After completing eight grades in the one-room, rural school near his home, David enrolled in Martinsburg Normal School, where he met the requirements for a state teacher's certificate. After two years of study at Shenandoah Collegiate Institute, he enrolled in Lebanon Valley College, graduating with a Bachelor of Arts degree in 1917. His studies for the ministry were completed at Bonebrake (now United) Seminary in 1920 and Virginia Conference ordained him elder that same year.[2]

A month before graduation from the seminary, the Board of Publication elected him associate editor of the *Religious Telescope*. The following year he became assistant to Dr. S. S.

Hough, the executive secretary of the Board of Administration and was assigned responsibility for directing the four million dollar United Enlistment Movement in the United Brethren Church.[3]

During his four years as president of Shenandoah College, the school was fully accredited as a junior college. In recognition of his leadership in education, Lebanon Valley College honored him with a Doctor of Divinity degree in 1924.[4] Thirty years later, both Albright College[5] and Otterbein College[6] awarded him honorary degrees.

Doctor Gregory began a ten-year pastorate at Euclid Avenue United Brethren Church in Dayton, Ohio, in the summer of 1926. The 1937 General Conference elected him executive secretary of the Board of Administration while he was serving as superintendent of Miami Conference. He became bishop in 1950.[7]

A glimpse of Bishop Gregory's pastoral ministry is seen in an incident related by Bishop Fred L. Dennis, who was Doctor Gregory's immediate predecessor at Euclid Avenue Church. He met one of the members on the street one day and inquired how the new pastor was being received. She responded by describing a pastoral call to her home:

When she answered the knock at the front door, Doctor Gregory introduced himself as the new pastor of her church. When he stepped inside while still standing with his hat in his hand, he said: "May I offer a prayer before we visit?" He asked God's blessing and guidance upon the members of that home and upon the visit that would take place. She then told her former pastor of the spiritual refreshment she and her family had received from that pastoral call.[8]

Bishop Gregory was known for his strong feelings about stewardship which he not only preached but practiced. He wrote a small book called *Stewardship the Key to Christian Service* which was used widely in Sunday schools. He was frequently asked to teach the biblical principles of stewardship in summer camps and district meetings. He wrote *The Minister and Local Church Finance* to assist pastors in developing effective and challenging biblical stewardship programs.

Bishop Gregory had the ability to share the depth and warmth of his faith in simple language that challenged his listeners. He once defined Christianity as "a way of life that is characterized by faithfully being something for Christ's sake and cheerfully doing something for the sake of one's fellowmen. It is not enough that those who accept Christ as Savior to be passively good. Christ calls his followers to a way of life that is good for something."[9]

One who was close to both Bishop and Mrs. Gregory described them as "sacrificial souls. They denied themselves to the point many were not able to understand. In the days of the great financial crisis of our Bonebrake Seminary in Dayton, Ohio, they mortgaged practically every earthly possession in order to save this institution, and at the same time, they shared half of their salary with the family of one of the seminary professors."[10]

While eating with a "soldier of rank" in a dining car one Saturday evening, the soldier asked Doctor Gregory, "Preacher, do you believe in God? Do you believe he answers prayers?" When Doctor Gregory assured him that he did, the officer said, "then pray for me and these boys as we go to war." Doctor Gregory said, "there at the table I prayed for him and the train load of young men, for which he thanked me."[11] This action was as instinctive for Bishop Gregory as it was for him to breathe.

The two separated at Pittsburgh and the officer said to him, "Preacher, I will be praying as we ride through the night that God will show you the man tomorrow whom you ought to lead to Christ in the city where you are going."

Upon Doctor Gregory's early morning arrival in the city, he said, "I saw a man intoxicated and with soiled clothing as a result of his night of carousal. The Spirit of God indicated to me, 'There is your man.' I engaged him in conversation as best I could and persuaded him to walk with me to the hotel. I tried to have him promise he would come to services during the day, but to no avail. He did, however, ask me if I would have supper with him and his family that evening and gave me his address.

"Late that afternoon," Doctor Gregory continued, "I took a cab and went to the address he had given. There I found all the evidence of a drunkard's home. With badly used silverware and from broken dishes, we ate bread and butter and drank water together. After the meal, we stood by a poorly improvised stove in what ought to have been a living room and talked about Jesus. There he finally reached out his hand and said as I gripped his hand, 'Preacher, it will be different from here on, for Jesus is moving in.'

"From that hour until his death, he lived a sober life and proved himself a blessing to his wife and children. When his widow later thanked me, I had to say, 'You owe me no thanks, good woman. Thank God for the soldier who rode through the night before I saw your husband, praying that God would show me the man I ought to lead to Christ while in your city.'"[12]

Doctor Gregory's secretary said of him, "He was a deeply spiritual man . . . humble, very sympathetic, and always cordial. He had a deep Christian perception."[13]

Bishop and Mrs. Gregory were killed instantly in a highway accident in Ohio, December 27, 1956, as they were traveling to their home in Pittsburgh after a Christmas visit with their daughter, Mrs. Thelma Jackson, in Dayton.

Funeral services were held on December 31 at Euclid Avenue Evangelical United Brethren Church in Dayton, Ohio, and on January 2 at St. Luke's Church in Martinsburg, West Virginia. Bishop Fred L. Dennis gave the memorial address at both services, and their bodies were buried in Rosedale Cemetery at Martinsburg.[14]

Bishop J. Gordon Howard said: "It would be impossible to list and commend all of the many virtues and admirable qualities which made Bishop Gregory so widely respected and greatly loved."[15]

NOTES

1. David T. Gregory, "Prayer" in *The Resources of the Church* (Dayton, Ohio: Otterbein Press, 1956), pp. 45, 46.
2. *Who Was Who in America* (Chicago: A. N. Marquis Company, 1968), Vol. 3 (1951-1968), p. 346.
3. *Telescope-Messenger* (January 19, 1957), p. 16.
4. Ibid.
5. Ibid (April 10, 1954), p. 12.
6. Ibid (May 22, 1954), p. 13.
7. *Proceedings of the Second General Conference of The Evangelical United Brethren Church* (Dayton, Ohio: Otterbein Press, 1950), p. 52.
8. As told to the author by Bishop Fred L. Dennis.
9. David T. Gregory, "The Challenge of His Call," *Telescope-Messenger*, Vol. 117 (September 22, 1951), p. 16.

10. Personal correspondence from Glenn E. Donelson to the author (December 19, 1972).
11. David T. Gregory, "Prayer" in *The Resources of the Church,* p. 47.
12. Ibid, pp. 47-48.
13. Personal correspondence from Mrs. Jean Weaver to the author (January 4, 1973).
14. *Telescope-Messenger* (January 19, 1957), p. 16.
15. David Franklin Glovier, *Pictorial History of the Virginia Conference* (Staunton, Virginia: McClure Printing Company, 1965), p. 133.

BISHOP REUBEN H. MUELLER

11

Always on the Road

Among Bishop Reuben H. Mueller's treasured mementos from more than a half century in the Christian ministry, is an illuminated manuscript in red and black lettering by a Chicago artist, presented to him by his Evangelical United Brethren colleagues upon completion of a three-year term as president of the National Council of Churches:[1]

Bishop Reuben Herbert Mueller
"I have been constantly on the road"
2 Corinthians 11:26
This text tells the story of three
fruitful years as president of the National
Council of Churches of Christ in the U.S.A.
1963-1966
This road by land, sea and air
was traveled with the courage of obedience
to Him who is the Way.
Adequacy for the journey came in
fulfillment of the promise: "My grace
is all you need"
The Board of Bishops
The Evangelical United Brethren Church
G. E. Epp

Harold R. Heininger	W. Maynard Sparks
J. Gordon Howard	Paul M. Herrick
Hermann W. Kaebnick	Paul W. Milhouse

"On the road" not only describes Bishop Mueller's years as president of the National Council of Churches, but all of his eighteen years as bishop. In addition to the travel involved as episcopal leader of the West Central Area of the church, extensive travel in Europe was required to give leadership to the conferences in Germany and Switzerland.

In 1971, Dr. Gustav Heinemann, on behalf of the government of West Germany, presented Reuben H. Mueller the Officer's Cross, First Class, Order of Merit. West Germany's highest award bestowed on civilians was given to the bishop in recognition of his "services to the Republic in strengthening our churches and supporting the ministry of hospitals and homes during the days of reconstruction" following World War II.[2]

"In one annual conference session in West Germany," he wrote, "I ordained nine ministers, everyone of whom had spent extended time in war imprisonment during World War II,

69

many in Russia." Not permitted to travel behind the Iron Curtain beyond East Berlin, he arranged for the pastors in East Germany to meet him in that city for conferences. "These first gatherings," he said, "particularly our first communion service together, were never-to-be-forgotten experiences in Christian love and fellowship."[3]

During his four years as bishop in the United Methodist Church following church union in 1968, Bishop Mueller made several trips to Europe to assist in uniting the Evangelical United Brethren and Methodist conferences.

Reuben Herbert Mueller, born June 2, 1897, in St. Paul, Minnesota, grew up in an Evangelical Church parsonage, the son of the Reverend Reinhold Michael Mueller and his wife, Emma Huldah Bunse Mueller, daughter of an Evangelical minister. Writing of his boyhood, Reuben said, "In our home the family altar was a daily experience, morning and evening, and we all took our turn at saying grace at the table. . . . Our father preached in German almost all of his 41 years. . . . In Sunday school all of us had to learn the German alphabet first and how to read German, so we could read the German Bible, sing the German hymns and understand the German sermons. . . ."[4]

In school, Reuben became involved in debating teams and public speaking classes. His American history teacher encouraged her pupils to organize parliamentary senates and courts of law. Reuben decided to become a lawyer and his father insisted that if he was going to be a lawyer, he wanted him to be "a good lawyer—honest, ethical and well prepared. That meant four years of college after high school and then law school."[5]

"At the age of 13, I confessed faith in Christ as my Savior and my surrender to Him as Lord of my whole life. This was a quiet, deliberate declaration . . . the reality of which I have never doubted. As the experience grew on me in the next several years, I became impressed with the idea that I ought to become a preacher."[6]

His probationer's license which he received on May 3, 1918, was signed by Bishop S. C. Breyfogel and by his father as secretary of the Minnesota Annual Conference. His certificate of ordination as elder, received four years later, carries the signature of his brother, H. E. Mueller, who was secretary of the Minnesota Conference at that time.

After spending two months of intensive training at Fort Sheridan, Illinois, during World War I, he was commissioned a second lieutenant and assigned to Ohio State University to drill students. Following the signing of the Armistice on November 11, he was discharged at the end of December and returned to North Central College, graduating with a Bachelor of Arts degree in June, 1919.

He accepted a teaching position in the New Richmond (Wisconsin) high school and on December 26, 1919, he and Magdalene Stauffacher, a teacher at Mineral Point, were married. The next year, he taught at Northwest School of Agriculture in Crookston, Minnesota, a branch of Minnesota University. Their daughter, Margaret, was born here. In April, 1921, the family moved to Minneapolis to establish a new congregation.

With intensive calling by both Reuben and Magdalene, Oakland Avenue Church was soon established and grew rapidly. Three years of teaching and trying to be pastor of a new congregation persuaded Reuben that he must be a preacher. "I knew that if this was to be, then I must have seminary training . . . . I knew that I needed a systematizing of my beliefs so that I could be consistent in teaching and preaching the whole gospel for the whole person and the whole world."

Reuben Mueller became pastor of Grace Evangelical Church in South Bend, Indiana, in 1924. "By 1926 we were building a new church and education structure, and I graduated from the seminary," writes Bishop Mueller. "The congregation was building up and attendance was growing steadily. A program of teaching (Christian education) and evangelism was developed in which the two were closely interwoven."[7]

After an eight-year pastorate at Grace Church and five years at First Evangelical Church in Indianapolis, he served as a district superintendent until elected general secretary of Christian Education and Evangelism in 1942. The 1954 General Conference selected him to serve as one of the episcopal leaders of the church.

Bishop Mueller has been a good administrator with ability to organize and lead people in achieving worthy goals. His creative mind has always been alert to new opportunities and pos-

71

sibilities. He knows how to "size up" a situation, identify its essential elements and propose effective action.

The bishop's ministry to the church and society has been recognized by honorary doctorate degrees from eight colleges and universities, including Union Theological Seminary in Tokyo. He received the Distinguished Alumnus Award from North Central College in 1964, the Upper Room Citation in 1967, Distinguished Medal of Honor from the University of Evansville in 1970 and the Medal of Honor from The Indiana Academy in 1971.

While president of the National Council of Churches, he made pre-Easter visits to United States armed forces in South Vietnam in 1963, in Spain and Germany in 1964, and in Japan, Korea and Taiwan in 1965. His work in World Christian Education has taken him to Toronto, Tokyo, Glasgow, Frankfurt, Oslo, Belfast, Mexico City, Nairobi and Lima. He served as a member of the Central Committee of the World Council of Churches for several years.

His episcopal residence was in Indianapolis during his 18 years as active bishop. Before 1968 church union, his area included Michigan and Ontario, in addition to Indiana. With the union of the Evangelical United Brethren and Methodist churches, his assignment was limited to Indiana. By January 1, 1969, the three Methodist and two Evangelical United Brethren conferences in Indiana were united into two conferences.

He is "courageous in taking firm positions on important issues . . . an ardent advocate of unity in Jesus Christ," is the way a coworker characterized Bishop Mueller.[8] He has been described by another as "a deeply dedicated Christian . . . impatient with half heartedness. . . ."[9]

A seminary classmate of Bishop Mueller's calls him "a man of indomitable spirit and will. Always fearless and forthright, he often said things in certain situations that desperately needed to be said. He is a forceful preacher and possesses a thorough knowledge of the church Discipline, as well as correct parliamentary procedures."[10]

"It is not given to every leading churchman who bears his witness through the complex and demanding channels of ecclesiastical organization to keep his vision as clearly focused on the essentials of the gospel as Bishop Mueller has been able to do," wrote Dr. R. H. Espy, General Secretary of the National Council of Churches.[11]

In writing of the church Bishop Mueller said, "No man ever dreamed up the church or laid out its plan on an architect's drawing board, or carried out the building of it. The church was born in the mind and heart of God before the beginning of time. . . . Much of the problem with reference to understanding the church and much of the basis of controversy about the church in our time can be laid directly to a misconception of the nature and character of the Church of Jesus Christ."[12]

Bishop Mueller has always insisted that "it is the purpose of Christian education to lead persons into the vital experience of faith in Jesus Christ as Savior and Lord and into living membership in His church. . . ."[13]

When questioned about the future of the church on one occasion, he said: "Tomorrow can never be independent of yesterday, but it ought never to be chained and manacled by the customs and methods of yesterday. Instead, the glowing response to the infilling of the Holy Spirit that characterized and empowered the church at Pentecost must needs become our experience today if tomorrow is to be a renewal of 'that great and notable day of the Lord' in which many shall be saved. That is our outstanding need."[14]

After retirement in 1972, Bishop and Mrs. Mueller moved to 133 West Franklin Avenue, Apartment 1, Naperville, Illinois.

NOTES

1. Biographical information received from R. H. Mueller at the author's request (May 14, 1973, and February 12, 1974).
2. Ibid.
3. Ibid.
4. Ibid.
5. Ibid.
6. Ibid.
7. Ibid.
8. Personal correspondence from L. L. Huffman to the author (January 29, 1973).
9. Personal correspondence from Arthur C. Core to the author (December 21, 1972).
10. Personal correspondence from Harley E. Hiller to the author (October 18, 1972).
11. R. H. Espy in the Introduction to R. H. Mueller's book, *His Church* (Nashville, Tennessee: Abingdon Press, 1966), p. 7.
12. Reuben H. Mueller, *His Church*, p. 13.
13. Ibid, p. 105.
14. Reuben H. Mueller, "Our Church Tomorrow," in *Facing Frontiers* (Dayton, Ohio: Otterbein Press, 1960), p. 64.

BISHOP H. R. HEININGER

12

I Promise to Preach His Word

On the first day of August in 1912, the following words were written in the diary of a seventeen-year-old boy: "I hereby pledge and give myself fully into the hands of the Lord and promise to do the work, by His help, which he gives me to do. More specifically, I promise to preach His word. I made my vow with God and by His help, I'll keep it. Stoutsville Camp. Signed, Harold Heininger."

"I often returned to this event to recognize a sense of direction and a reproducible experience of cleansing and forgiveness," said Bishop Heininger. "From that day forward, many subsequent decisions awaited me. The venture from there into the future held many unexpected developments, but there was an abiding sense of belonging to Him who holds the future."[1]

When Harold was granted license to preach, he became the third generation of Heiningers to enter the ministry of the Evangelical Church. Like his father and grandfather before him, his ministry continued through more than half a century.

Harold Rickel Heininger laughs as he tells about his birth in a hotel room. His parents, the Reverend John Wesley and Ida Luella Rickel Heininger were on their way from Elwood, Indiana, to their new assignment in Ohio. They planned to stop with Mrs. Heininger's parents near Ashland, Ohio, until after the birth of their child, but "they miscalculated my arrival," said the bishop. "At Lima, Ohio, they found it necessary to leave the train and rush mother to a hotel where I was born."[2] The date was August 13, 1895.

Following graduation from high school, Harold enrolled in Adelbert College of Western Reserve University from which he was graduated with Bachelor of Arts degree in 1917. After 15 months in the United States Army during World War I, he was honorably discharged with the rank of First Lieutenant of Infantry.

On January 1, 1919, he became an assistant on the staff of Calvary Evangelical Church in Cleveland with responsibilities also related to the Cleveland Federation of Churches. After Calvary congregation recommended him for license to preach, Harold enrolled in Evangelical Theological Seminary at Naperville, Illinois. There he met Erma Martin whom he married on his birthday, August 13, 1925.

He described his first meeting with Erma in this manner: "I

was playing tennis across the street from the seminary when a friend asked my assistance in moving the trunks of four young ladies from one rooming house . . . to another. . . . They were freshmen at North Western (now North Central) College. . . . I was not especially eager to have my game interrupted, and I was less so when I learned that he proposed to use a wheelbarrow in moving them.

"I consented, however. After we had struggled to get the last one down the stairs, I heard a sweet voice calling down, 'Wouldn't you care for some fudge?' This we could not resist, so we went back upstairs, and that was how I first met Erma Martin."[3]

In order to meet expenses at Boston University where Harold enrolled after graduation from seminary, he worked in a restaurant for his meals and served as pastor of a small congregation in the cotton mill city of Fall River, Massachusetts.

Of his study there he said, "The professors at Boston University School of Theology saw to it that the academic horizons were pushed back and disciplined study of our faith and its history required. . . . I qualified the first year for the degree Bachelor of Sacred Theology and the second year for the degree Master of Sacred Theology."[4]

In the fall of 1923, he accepted a position on the faculty of Evangelical Theological Seminary. While here, he did research work at the University of Chicago and wrote a dissertation on the theological methods of Horace Bushnell in meeting requirements for his Doctor of Philosophy degree in 1933. Doctor Heininger was elected president of the seminary in 1939. One of the guest books kept by Doctor and Mrs. Heininger during their association with the seminary contains 556 signatures of overnight guests from the United States and twelve other countries during a period of less than six years. Bishop Heininger said, "Those were years when we lacked good restaurants in Naperville. I could call Erma at 11:30 and ask to bring home a luncheon guest. She had a special recipe that she could toss together in a hurry, and shortly after twelve we would sit down to a nice meal."[5]

In 1954, Harold Heininger was elected bishop and assigned to residence in Minneapolis to serve an area that included Illinois, Wisconsin, Minnesota, North and South Dakota and

Northwest Canada. Commenting upon his travel experience over the area, he said, "I learned how men dress for 40 degrees below zero in Northwest Canada and how the chinook wind earned its reputation as the snow eater."[6]

Referring to his work as bishop, he wrote, "I learned how to listen to pastors, to lay people, and to conference superintendents. I studied Robert's Rules of Order and the church Discipline. . . . Ordinations never lost their high significance for me as young men presented themselves after meeting the requirements this high office called for and took the solemn vows involved. . . . I learned to trust the promise, 'As thy days so shall thy strength be' and to come back again and again to the text I tried to use in 1921 in my seminary chapel sermon, 'For we are laborers together with God.' The records indicate that 245 men were ordained in the conferences in the United States and Canada and in Europe, over which I served as chairman from 1955 to 1968."[7]

The extensive travel which has accompanied all of Bishop Heininger's long ministry is reflected in this comment: "When celebrating our forty-fifth wedding anniversary, I made the remark that it was wonderful to have lived together for so many years. My lady picked up the remark and said, 'Yes, it has been wonderful to have been married for forty-five years, but we have not lived together that long a time!' Her reference, of course, was to my frequent absences from home in connection with my work as professor and president of the seminary and later as a bishop of the church.

"This conversation stimulated a research project for her in her carefully kept diary since she was in high school to determine exactly how much absenteeism on my part had been in the record. She later reported her findings. . . . The total for the forty-five years (1925-1970) was nine years, seven months and twenty-six nights."[8]

Bishop Heininger has always paid high tribute to his wife who has shared in his ministry, "She has exemplified, across the years, the creative significance of Christian womanhood. Her career has been that of homemaker. . . . Her profound Christian faith, nurtured in the fellowship of her home church in Webster, New York, and in her years in college at Naperville, found multiple ways of witnessing, without fanfare or public relations publicity. Her husband was supposed to be teaching Christian theology. She lived it."[9]

Upon retirement in 1968, the Heiningers moved to 133 West Franklin Street, Apartment 7, Naperville, Illinois. On Sunday afternoon, August 3, 1969, they were honored at a reception in the Community United Methodist Church in Naperville in recognition of Bishop Heininger's 50 years in the Christian ministry. A fellow churchman said of the bishop, "He is loved, admired and respected by all who know him as a Christian gentleman, a scholar and an inspiring Christian leader."[10]

Bishop Heininger, always able to see the humorous side of any event, described the clean-up of his ruined library in this manner: "Good storage space in the basement of this apartment was one of the strong points stressed in the renting of our four small rooms on the second floor . . . many of my choice volumes rested in this basement and must have felt neglected although they were dry and protected. . . . Each book was treasured in one way or another. Each had its halo of memories and cluster of associations accumulated across thirty-two years of teaching and an additional fourteen years of administration. Each volume had a personal biography of its own. . . . Then last Friday night the cloud burst came to the DuPage County, Illinois, with its torrential rain whipped by high winds one inch per hour . . . new ponds were born and lakes appeared. Dry basements became swimming pools. . . . The dry storage space in our basement joined the parade and became a pool. . . . My library should be listed among the flood casualties. . . .

"The big boxes underneath, when soaked, collapsed. This permitted the huge cartons on the top to tumble in a confused pyramid of heavy sections poised in mid-air on their way to the floor. As soon as possible old clothes became the uniform of the day and a team of man and wife tackled the awesome and odoriferous task of problem solving which required more brawn than brain.

"The funeral for the departed was emotionally charged at every step in the ritual. The old wash-day basket was lined with plastic. The smelly, saturated, beloved books, one by one, were reverently placed in this plastic, decorated conveyance and carted with much groaning and puffing (with rest periods at stated intervals) to the refuse bins . . . fourteen steps up from the basement to daylight, and fourteen steps down again for the next load. . . . We lifted them tenderly as pall bearers might. We dumped them prayerfully into the huge receptacle with a sincere and silent benediction, 'Rest in Peace.'"[11]

These lines taken from the Heiningers' 1973 Christmas greetings reflect their radiant faith which has always been kept "up to date:"

"News Not in the Headlines!

"In the Middle East a baby was born in Bethlehem, Judea. The child's name is Jesus—Savior—Immanuel, which means 'God is with us!' There is hope for our troubled world—Christ is born! There is a cure for what is wrong with human nature —Christ is born! Good news for disillusioned America—Christ is born! Glad tidings for discouraged Christians—Christ is born! Because 'God loved the world so much that he gave his only Son that everyone who has faith in Him may not die but have eternal life'—NOW!

HALLELUJAH!

NOTES

1. Biographical information provided the author by Harold R. Heininger (February 10, 1973), pp. 5, 6.
2. Ibid, p. 5.
3. "Bishop Heininger, Observing 50 Years in Christian Ministry," *The Naperville Sun* (July 24, 1969), p. 5.
4. Biographical information provided by Harold R. Heininger, pp. 17-18.
5. "Bishop Heininger, Observing 50 Years in Christian Ministry," *The Naperville Sun* (July 24, 1969), p. 6. .
6. Biographical information provided by Harold R. Heininger, p. 22.
7. Ibid, pp. 22-23.
8. Ibid, pp. 26-27.
9. Ibid, p. 29
10. Personal correspondence from L. L. Huffman to the author (January 29, 1973).
11. Biographical information provided by Harold R. Heininger (September 1, 1972).

BISHOP L. L. BAUGHMAN

13

He Believed in
Church-Centered Stewardship

During the depression of the thirties when jobs were hard to find and money was scarce, the young pastor of a United Brethren Church in northern Illinois became widely known for challenging church members to demonstrate their faith in God by giving ten cents out of each dollar earned to the church, which he called the modern equivalent of "storehouse" mentioned in Malachi 3:10—"Bring the full tithes into the storehouse, that there may be food in my house, and thereby put me to the test, says the Lord of hosts, if I will not open the windows of heaven for you and pour down for you an overflowing blessing."

He developed *A Unified Church-Centered Financial System* as a practical, scripturally based channel which the individual could use for sending his dollars on Christian errands of mercy and mission through the church and to agencies beyond the church. While many churches were floundering on financial rocks at low tide, this pastor's church and others which had adopted his plan had sufficient financial resources to carry on an effective and far-reaching ministry. This pastor was Lyle Lynden Baughman.

Lyle, born April 5, 1899, in Cuba, Illinois, was the youngest of five children in the family of Joseph Eli and Eva Stonemets Baughman.[1] He became a member of the Smithfield United Brethren Church and while still in high school, expressed conviction that he felt called to the Christian ministry. He was approved for license to preach on December 25, 1916. At that time he was serving as pastor of two nearby congregations, Shields and Locust Lane, and continued there until 1924. He was received into the Illinois Conference in 1917; and after graduation from Canton high school in 1919, he continued study under the direction of Bonebrake (now United) Theological Seminary to complete the course of study then prescribed by the United Brethren Church Discipline.[2]

On June 7, 1922, Lyle and Fern Edna Brock, a school teacher, were married in Peoria, Illinois. He was ordained elder in 1923 by Bishop H. H. Fout and the next year was appointed pastor of Saybrook United Brethren Church, remaining there until 1932 when he was assigned to First Church in Bloomington. During this 13-year pastorate, Lyle Baughman became recognized as an aggressive leader who "got things done."

Indiana Central College honored him with a Doctor of Divinity degree in 1938. When Illinois Conference elected him superintendent in 1945, he brought to his new task the same hard work and careful planning that had been evident in his pastorates. He presented his goals with persuasive enthusiasm and suggested procedures for attaining them. He took little time for hobbies although he enjoyed music, painting, gardening and photography.[3]

The church recognized his ability as a leader by electing him executive secretary of the General Council of Administration in 1950.[4] The next General Conference chose him to serve as bishop in Kansas City to supervise the conferences of the Southwestern Area.[5]

Dr. Stanley B. Williams, who served in the Southwestern Area for 23 years as Home Missions and Church Extension executive, said of Bishop Baughman and his work: "The Southwestern Area, as I have known it, never had a more utterly dedicated leader. He always did a prodigious amount of research and preparation in outlining the program which he desired his conference leaders and pastors to carry out and gave to the prosecution of the task every ounce of energy he possessed. Next to Bishop Weekly, he was the most evangelistic of the line of bishops who have served this area. He appeared never to carry so many burdens that he was not willing to take on another if requested to do so. Perhaps his greatest contribution to this area, and for that matter the whole church, was in the field of Christian stewardship."[6]

Bishop Baughman was sent to Sierra Leone, West Africa, to preside over the conference there in 1958 and again in 1960. He also visited Ceylon, Nigeria and Europe. Upon his return, he shared his observations with the conferences of his area.[7] He was proud of the gavel presented to him by the Sierra Leone Conference.[8]

Believing it important to teach the principles of Christian stewardship to children, he wrote: "An important phase of stewardship is sharing our possessions with the Lord. The child should be trained in expressing his gratitude to God through his gifts. If the giving of children is to have the deepest meaning, the total work of the church should be included and the total budget of the church should be presented on their level of understanding. The children have a right to know the extensive outreach of the church."[9]

He believed that "first century Christianity survived and thrived because of the enlistment and practice of stewardship," and when "there was a lapse from the New Testament quality of stewardship emphasis and practice . . . the church tended toward authority and formalism instead of spiritual experience and partnership with God."[10]

In a letter to members of the Kansas Annual Conference, he wrote, "We are called to awareness that our inner spiritual life determines the quality of our witness, service and outreach. A Christian and a congregation of growing power come out of deepening and growing experiences with the Lord. The cross is our symbol and not a cushion. We are called to be alert, and not inert. Our sufficiency is of God, who makes us able servants of the new covenant."[11]

During the period of his episcopal leadership, the former Evangelical and United Brethren conferences of the area were united in their respective states. A layman said: "It was his dynamic leadership that finally brought the two Kansas annual conferences together."[12] Westmar College recognized his effective leadership with an honorary Doctor of Laws degree in 1957.

A denominational executive said Bishop Baughman was "a man of great energy, always giving meticulous attention to details. He always did his 'homework' with great thoroughness. He came to the board meetings well prepared."[13]

On Sunday evening, May 15, 1960, he and his wife stopped at a motel in Wellington, Kansas, on their way to Oklahoma where he was to preside over the Oklahoma-Texas Conference. It had been a strenuous day, preaching the closing sermon at the Kansas Conference that morning and dedicating a new church building that afternoon. While watching television, he slumped over in his chair and died at about 10 o'clock that evening.[14]

Funeral services were conducted from Trinity Evangelical United Brethren Church in Kansas City, Missouri, on Wednesday morning, May 18. The body was taken to Canton, Illinois, for a second service with burial in the Baughman Cemetery near Smithfield.

Bishop R. H. Mueller, who gave the sermon at both services, said, "I have discovered that it was not only the tireless application to the task at hand nor the drive of this man that caused others to follow him in serving Christ, it was the quality of his devotion to Christ, the sincerity of his dedication, the undivided loyalty to Christ. . . . He was a Christian gentleman."[15]

The bishop's last sermon was preached to the Kansas Conference based on Ephesians 2:13-22. He began by saying, "We have had high moments. We have seen democracy at work this week. Let us join in prayer that this will be a climactic service to send us out to fulfill His purpose."[16]

A superintendent said it well. "He preached with fervor and served his God and his church with distinction."[17]

NOTES

1. *Who Was Who in America* (Chicago: A. N. Marquis Company, 1968), Vol. 4 (1961-1968), p. 65.
2. Personal correspondence from Mrs. L. L. Baughman to the author (July 30, 1972).
3. Ibid.
4. *Proceedings of the Second General Conference of The Evangelical United Brethren Church* (Dayton, Ohio: Otterbein Press, 1950), p. 66.
5. *Proceedings of the Third General Conference of The Evangelical United Brethren Church* (Dayton, Ohio: Otterbein Press, 1954), p. 66.
6. Stanley B. Williams, *The Southwestern Area as I have Know It* (Kansas City: Kansas Conference, Evangelical United Brethren Church, 1968), p. 60.
7. *Kansas Conference Bulletin* (June, 1958, and July, 1960).
8. Ibid (June, 1959).
9. *The Telescope-Messenger* (Harrisburg, Pennsylvania: May 22, 1954), p. 16.
10. Ibid. (May 1, 1954), p. 14.
11. *Kansas Conference Bulletin* (May, 1960).
12. Personal correspondence from Clem H. Ewald to the author (August 29, 1972).
13. Personal correspondence from H. E. Hiller to the author (October 18, 1972).
14. *Kansas Conference Bulletin* (June, 1960).
15. *The Telescope-Messenger* (June 11, 1960), p. 15.
16. Kansas Conference Bulletin (July, 1960).
17. Personal correspondence from H. H. Vogel to the author (October 3, 1972).

BISHOP PAUL E. SHANNON

14

An Altar Was Dedicated in His Memory

The records of Lebanon Valley College indicate that in 1958, "the ministerial student society, Delta Tau Chi, aided by the East Pennsylvania Conference and the Pennsylvania Conference presented to the college an altar for the prayer corner in the Gossard Memorial Library dedicated by Bishop George E. Epp in memory of the late Bishop Paul E. V. Shannon, '18, who had been a devoted friend of the college. The corner is now in daily use for prayer and meditation."[1]

No other memorial could have been as appropriate for one whose whole-hearted devotion to God enabled him to walk through many valleys of sorrow and tragedy with faith unshaken and his spirit untainted by bitterness or complaint.

The Reverend Absalom Lincoln and Linnie Erb Shannon, living in the United Brethren parsonage at Mountville, Pennsylvania, welcomed the birth of their fifth child on March 25, 1898, with the dream that he would become a minister in the church they loved and served. They named him after the Apostle Paul and Eugene Field, whose writings they enjoyed. Fifteen years later, his mother added Virgil to his name.

His parents planned for Paul and his brother Carl to attend Lebanon Valley College where they had first met, but circumstances began to develop that cast a shadow over such dreams. Before Paul was three years of age, his father died of diphtheria just twelve days before Christmas, leaving very little financial resources for Paul's mother to care for her six children. She worked at whatever jobs were available, but the long hours away from home and the care of the children proved to be too much. Four of the children were placed in other homes. Paul and his invalid sister, Lois, remained with the mother.

Their hand-to-mouth existence meant there were days without food. Lois, who suffered from a heart ailment, died while still a young teenager. One month before Paul's graduation from high school, his mother died. He wrote: "I was called into the room and there was my mother drawing her last breath. She had laid down her life for us as the Good Shepherd did. Worldly separation is cruel, yet we can be thankful that we can not fully realize our loss. I immediately placed my heart in God's will and said, 'Thy will be done'"[2] This marked his decision to enter the gospel ministry.

Paul and Carl lived together after their mother's death; and when they inherited a little money from an aunt, they enrolled in Lebanon Valley College. After receiving license to preach, Paul was appointed pastor of two churches near Middletown, Pennsylvania. Under the combined load of college studies and pastoral responsibilities, he suffered a physical breakdown. This was the first of several that plagued his ministry, but there was never any expression of bitterness or self pity. Of this occasion, he later wrote, "I was not worried or frightened for I knew the Lord would provide for his own, and he surely did."[3]

In order to attend college, it was necessary for Paul to work during the summer and at other times whenever possible. One summer he secured a job at the steel mill in Steelton, Pennsylvania. His first day on the job was spent cracking limestone rocks with a heavy sledge hammer. By evening his hands were raw and bloody and his muscles ached so that the pain kept him awake most of the night, but he was back on the job the next morning without a complaint.

When the foreman expressed surprise that he had returned, Paul explained his need to earn money for college expenses. The foreman bandaged his hands and transferred him to easier work. When the summer job had to be relinquished to return to school, the foreman, who spoke in broken English, said to Paul, "Me think me cry a little bit."[4]

Following graduation from Lebanon Valley in 1918 at twenty years of age, Paul spent the summer as pastor of the United Brethren Church in Veedersburg, Indiana. In September he enrolled in Bonebrake (now United) Theological Seminary in Dayton, Ohio. The following summer, he was married to Josephine Mathias, to whom he had become engaged while in college.

During the second year in seminary, he began serving as pastor of Fairview Church, but ill health later forced him out of the pulpit. In his farewell message to Fairview congregation he said: "It is no compliment to a pastor to have his work fail in his absence. I have tried to win you to Christ. If I have succeeded, you will be faithful; if I have won you to myself, then the church will fail. The biggest compliment you can pay me is to carry on the work for which I have given my strength."[5]

Two days before Christmas in 1924, the Shannon Family moved to a cottage at Mt. Gretna, Pennsylvania. Here they struggled for survival. Illness sometimes kept Paul in bed for weeks at a time. Of these 15 months at Mt. Gretna, he wrote, "I have often thanked the Lord for that experience. It made me a better man. It gave me more sympathy and understanding for others in trouble."[6]

With recovery of health in early 1926, he was assigned to the Liberty Heights section of Baltimore to establish a new congregation. After 15 months of ministry there, it seemed wise to abandon the project. He then spent time soliciting funds and students for the Seminary, and in 1928, was appointed pastor of Bethlehem Church in Dallastown, Pennsylvania. During the 1931 annual conference session, his wife died. Her father had moved into the parsonage earlier and now became baby sitter for the girls while Paul carried out his pastoral duties. The next year Grandpa Mathias died of a heart attack.

That summer was spent at Mt. Gretna campgrounds with Paul's brother, Carl, and his wife and daughter. There he again met Katherine Higgins, a member of the Higgins Sisters Quartette. Paul and Katherine were married in November, 1932. Three years later, Paul Shannon became pastor of First United Brethren Church in York, where he served for thirteen years before being elected conference superintendent. Lebanon Valley College honored him with a Doctor of Divinity degree in 1937.

In 1957, he was elected bishop by mail ballot to fill the vacancy created by the death of Bishop D. T. Gregory. Continuing his responsibilities as superintendent until a successor could be elected, he took over the episcopal duties with his characteristic dedicated enthusiasm and whole-hearted commitment, but the pressure and strain of the additional work was more than his body could take. Lowered resistance led to an attack of strep throat that sent him to the doctor upon his arrival in Johnstown, Pennsylvania, for his first annual conference. He spent the third day of the conference in bed but returned to close the conference, and on Saturday, drove alone to his home in York.

On Sunday, he visited two small churches for dedication services. In response to his wife's request to ask some conference official to take his place, he replied: "I can't let down these two small churches. To visit them will be my last official act in this conference."[7]

He felt discomfort in his chest after the noon meal and consulted a doctor. On his return to York, his doctor sent him to the hospital. He died there on Thursday morning, May 23, 1957, the day on which a reception had been planned to honor him as bishop.

Funeral services were conducted at First Evangelical United Brethren Church in York on Sunday, May 26. Bishop George E. Epp preached the sermon. Burial was in the home cemetery in Dallastown, Pennsylvania, one block from the church he served for seven years.

The strength of his leadership in the Evangelical United Brethren Church was not from length of service but in the quality of his life and the impact of his unwaivering faith.

NOTES

1. Paul A. W. Wallace, *Lebanon Valley College: A Centennial History* (Annville, Pennsylvania: Lebanon Valley College, 1966), p. 233.
2. Personal correspondence from Bishop J. Gordon Howard to the author, containing biographical information on Paul Eugene Virgil Shannon compiled with the assistance of his widow (now Mrs. Howard) and his oldest daughter, Mrs. Jomarie Shannon Dresel (March 30, 1973).
3. Ibid.
4. Ibid.
5. Ibid.
6. Ibid.
7. Ibid.

BISHOP J. GORDON HOWARD

15

A Lamplighter

Bishop J. Gordon Howard earned his first money working as a lamplighter for the city of Dayton, Ohio. Each evening he walked three miles in Dayton View to light the 65 street lamps along his route and early each morning, retraced his steps to turn them off.[1]

He spent two years lighting the street lamps of his city, but has given a lifetime to lighting lamps of Christian faith through four careers: youth director, editor, college president and bishop.

John Gordon Howard was born in Tokyo, Japan, December 3, 1899, where his parents, Alfred and May Day Stevenson Howard, were serving as missionaries of the United Brethren Church. He lived there until he was twelve years of age, except for two years during the Russian-Japanese War.

"Upon our return to Japan in 1905," Gordon recalls, "there were great public celebrations following the Japanese victory over the Russians. I attended many of these parades and as a boy was quite thrilled by the marching soldiers, the long lines of cavalry horses and the big guns of the artillery. The victorious generals rode in bright red lacquer carriages drawn by six white horses. . . .

"On rare occasions there would be a parade in honor of the Emperor Meiji. He would come by in an open carriage with many horses and with outriders on horseback. The Emperor was regarded as a semi-divine character. The Japanese were forbidden to look at him. As he passed by, all the Japanese crowded along both sides of the street would bow low and never look at their ruler. As a typical American boy, I had no such reverence for the Emperor, so I would keep my head up and look directly at His Majesty."[2]

Gordon was guided through the first four grades of school by his mother. "For a schoolroom for my brother Don and myself, we used two small desks in our dining room. We used textbooks from Dayton, Ohio, schools. . . . For my fifth year . . . I attended a school in Tokyo operated by an Englishman for non-Japanese boys and girls. . . . My sixth and seventh grades . . . were in an American-style school operated by several American and Canadian missionary mothers. My mother was in charge of curriculum and textbooks. . . . My days as a boy in Japan were happy for the most part. However, Japanese children often showed their dislike for me as a little foreigner . . . sometimes called me obscene names."[3]

Gordon was in the eighth grade when the Howard family left Japan. Upon their return to Dayton, Ohio, the family became identified with the First United Brethren Church, and Gordon's relationship with this congregation continued for 32 years.

While attending Otterbein College from which his parents graduated in 1894, Gordon participated in dramatics, the Philophronean Literary Society, tennis, football and did some reporting for the local newspaper.

"During my senior year, I could not shake off the feeling that I should go into some form of religious work," he said. "My early days as a 'missionary kid' and the influence of my home could not be ignored. The thought came to me that perhaps I could combine my journalistic interest with a religious vocation. . . . As I look back on it now, this was my call."[4]

He enrolled at Bonebrake (now United) Theological Seminary in the fall of 1922, a year after his father became president of that institution. While studying church history, Gordon became disillusioned with the church because the historical facts did not correspond with his idealistic concept of the church. "My old urge for secular journalism began to reassert itself. I shared my doubts with Rhea McConaughy, my fiancee, and she listened patiently over a period of months. I wrote to three newspapers and received offers from two . . . but Rhea urged me to give the seminary another try for one more year. This I did and I never had occasion to regret my decision."[5]

On July 24, 1924, he and Rhea McConaughy were married, and during his third year in seminary he was part-time field secretary of the Sunday School and Christian Endeavor Union of Miami Conference. This position involved visiting churches on Sundays to promote Christian education.

"Dr. J. Harmon Dutton, the conference superintendent, was very helpful," says Gordon. "He would take me along on his church visitations. . . . I learned how helpful and educational a friendly relationship can be between an older and younger man in an informal setting. In later years in my counseling with others, I have always tried to keep the atmosphere as informal and unofficial as possible."[6]

Following graduation from the seminary in 1925, Gordon became an assistant to Dr. S. S. Hough in the General Board of Administration. This gave opportunity for writing and editing promotional leaflets and articles for church publications.

He went to New York University and Biblical Seminary for further study in the field of religious education, receiving a Masters degree in June, 1927. His dissertation was on "Martin Luther as an Educator."

Plans for continued study toward a doctorate were changed when he was invited to return to Dayton as director of young people's work.

Gordon speaks of his youth work as "one of the most pleasing experiences in my life." During this time, he wrote a column for the weekly youth church paper and two books, *The Successful Sunday School* and *When Youth Worships.* In 1940, he became associate editor of Sunday school literature and the next year was elected editor-in-chief. He wrote another book in 1942 entitled, *A Catechism for Youth.*

"Early in 1945, Dr. J. Ruskin Howe resigned the presidency of Otterbein College, and to my amazement," writes Bishop Howard, "I was asked if I would consider the presidency of my alma mater. I was very happy as an editor. I let it be known that I would not meet with the committee seeking a new president, I would not meet with the executive committee of the College Board of Trustees, and I would not meet the Board of the Trustees as a whole. But if these several bodies would vote on me favorably without my making any effort on my part to obtain the position as president, I would accept. This was a kind of 'Gideon's fleece' test on my part to see if this was really what I ought to do and in accord with the will of God."[7]

On May 4, 1945, the Board of Trustees of Otterbein College elected him president. In reflecting on his years at the college, Bishop Howard said, "As I think of it, the most notable contribution I made to Otterbein as college president was to involve students intimately and responsibly in the administration of everyday life on the campus. We established a Campus Roundtable which was made up of representative students who met regularly to consider problems of every kind. It was my theory, substantiated in practice, that if you give students all the facts, give them time to think things over and then motivate them sufficiently, nine times out of ten or oftener than that, they will come up with the right answers."[8]

On August 1, 1957, J. Gordon Howard was elected bishop by mail ballot to fill the vacancy created through the death of Bishop Paul E. V. Shannon and was assigned to residence in Pittsburgh with supervision over Western Pennsylvania, Erie, New York, West Virginia, Virginia, and Florida annual conferences. Upon the death of Bishop L. L. Baughman in 1960, the Sierra Leone Conference was added to Bishop Howard's responsibility.

"This Sierra Leone assignment had sentimental connections for me," wrote Bishop Howard, "inasmuch as my parents had gone to Sierra Leone as missionaries 66 years before, in 1894, and served for four years. . . . My wife, Rhea, and I visited Sierra Leone in January, 1961. . . . A few persons remembered my father and mother, and quite a few had known my father when he visited Sierra Leone as the missionary bishop of the United Brethren Church from 1913 to 1921."[9] Bishop Howard visited Sierra Leone six times during the next nine years.

Rhea died on July 18, 1964, just four days short of their fortieth wedding anniversary. Bishop Howard said, "Death came at 3 a.m. I was sitting beside her. When I realized she was no longer breathing, I was utterly desolated. Rhea was a superior wife and mother. She made a noble career of wifehood and motherhood."

Mrs. Howard's body was buried in Memorial Park Cemetery in Dayton, Ohio, beside the grave of their infant daughter who had died 34 years earlier.

Bishop Howard lived alone in the episcopal residence until February 9, 1967, when he married Katherine Higgins Shannon, the widow of Bishop Paul E. V. Shannon. In 1968, he was assigned to the Philadelphia Area of the United Methodist Church where he served until retiring to Winchester, Virginia, in 1972. He and Mrs. Howard live at 437 Imperial Street.

"I am trying to catch up on delayed reading," Bishop Howard writes from Winchester, "and am doing some systematic Bible study which has been long neglected while I was forced to concentrate on administrative duties."[10]

Bishop Howard had an unusual relationship to church union. He served as secretary of the Commission on Church

Union that brought together the Evangelical Church and United Brethren Church to form the Evangelical United Brethren Church in 1946. He served as a member of the Commission on Church Union that united the Evangelical United Brethren Church and the Methodist Church to establish the United Methodist Church in 1968.

Bishop Howard has always been able to face the realism of the present with the Christian's vision of what ought to be. In speaking to a General Convention of the Evangelical United Brethren Church, he said: "It would be dangerous to state that this is the worst stage of human history, but it is our stage—the day we have to use. It is incredible that we would sit around and do nothing."[11]

A district superintendent summed up the bishop's active ministry very well when he said, "He sought out people who seemed to be short on friends. He took time to engage them in conversation and took a personal interest in them. He was a good administrator . . . excellent presiding officer . . . had a great spirit of kindness . . . the most thoughtful individual I ever met . . . had a good balance between humor and seriousness."[12]

NOTES

1. Biographical information provided by J. Gordon Howard to the author (March 19, 1973).
2. Ibid.
3. Ibid.
4. Ibid.
5. Ibid.
6. Ibid.
7. Ibid.
8. Ibid
9. Ibid.
10 Personal correspondence from J. Gordon Howard to the author (October 26, 1972).
11. *The Telescope-Messenger* (August 8, 1960), p. 12.
12. Personal correspondence from Glenn E. Donelson to the author (December 19, 1972).

BISHOP H. W. KAEBNICK

16

God Wants You for the Ministry

Following the signing of the Armistice on November 11, 1918, that brought an end to fighting in World War I and his subsequent discharge from the United States Navy, Hermann W. Kaebnick enrolled in the Warren Conservatory of Music. For the next four years he "was submerged and enthralled with great classical music, composition, oratorio work, recitals and enriching experiences in church music. But always there was that inner, inescapable sense of 'call' to the ministry," he writes. "No matter what I did to distract or digress, the needle of that compass always swung back to the call: 'God wants you for the ministry.' In 1922, in response to the invitation of Bishop Samuel P. Spreng, I yielded and was examined by him and licensed to the Christian ministry at the annual session of the old Erie Conference of the Evangelical Association."

Hermann Walter Kaebnick's parents, Julius Frederick and Caroline Bloedow Kaebnick, were reared in Christian homes and educated in the schools of Germany where the Bible had a central place in the curriculum. When they migrated to the United States with their five children in 1890, they settled in Brookston, Pennsylvania, a community of about seventy-five German families. Hermann was born here February 13, 1898, and taken to the church altar for Christian baptism when he was four weeks old.

He was not yet two when his father died from pneumonia which he contracted while working in the sleet and snow to erect a new church building in the community of Brookston. Five years later, desiring a church that offered better Christian education opportunities for her children than was possible at Brookston where a pastor came once a month to preach, his mother moved the family to Warren so they could attend the Salem Evangelical Church.

"At seven years of age," said Hermann, "I came under the influence of trained school teachers, saintly ministers and a community whose influences contributed greatly to a pure, high-minded, wholesome youth life. Friendships were formed which have endured until the march of time has removed many of them by death."

When eleven, Hermann attended an after-school youth service that left a lasting impact upon his life. He said: "I shall never forget that day or that experience even though it has been sixty-four years ago. In all subsequent years that experience has been the compass which has held me true to the Christian course despite many trials and testings. . . . With my life commitment to Christ as Savior and Lord, I sensed a deep call to the ministry. While I never wavered in my Christian discipleship, I did not think the ministry was for me. There was my brother Ernest who could speak much more fluently in public than I, who could pray so much more effectively and meet people with great ease and grace. But I? the ministry? Oh, no!"

After receiving license to preach in 1922, Hermann began serious preparation for the ministry. He received his Bachelor of Arts degree from Central University in 1926, the Bachelor of Divinity degree from the Evangelical School of Theology (now United Theological Seminary) and Master of Sacred Theology from Lutheran Theological Seminary. He did further study at Yale, New York Theological Seminary, and the University of Pittsburgh.

Hermann and Gertrude Strehler, daughter of Reverend and Mrs. L. T. Strehler, were married August 4, 1927, and the following year, he was ordained an elder in the Evangelical Church. His service as pastor included Forest Hills Mission on Long Island and Freedom, Altoona and Somerset, Pennsylvania.

In each congregation which he served, he conducted week-day religious instruction classes, had well-organized groups with meaningful programs that included stewardship, evangelism, music and full payment of financial obligations to the conference and general church program. He held himself rigorously to a schedule of at least 1000 pastoral calls each year in addition to hospital calls.

Pastor Kaebnick disciplined himself to sixteen hours of preparation for each sermon. His summers were spent in gathering material for his preaching. He said: "When I planned a series of expository sermons on certain books of the Bible, I would read widely and 'dig' for source data that sometimes did not result in the kind of sermon I had wanted. I can count thirty Bible books out of the sixty-six which were thus treated in a series of sermons. . . . While my emphasis changed somewhat in what I found my congregation needed . . . . I tried to keep the emphasis in what I believed the word of God revealed."

In 1939, Hermann Kaebnick was elected superintendent of Western Pennsylvania Conference. The 1950 General Conference chose him as treasurer for the Evangelical United Brethren Church with office in Dayton, Ohio. Dedicated to his Lord and the church, he took special courses at the University of Dayton in order to be better prepared for his new responsibility. In 1954, he was made executive secretary of the General Council of Administration.

Mrs. Kaebnick died while the family lived in Dayton. He said: "When my wife of almost thirty years died, I must say that the loss was indescribably heavy, but I was sustained by the presence of God and the priceless memories and eternal hopes."

Elected bishop on the first ballot by the 1958 General Conference, he was assigned to residence in Harrisburg, Pennsylvania, to succeed retiring Bishop George E. Epp. His leadership in the church was recognized by Albright College honoring him with a Doctor of Laws degree in 1960, by Lycoming College granting him an honorary Doctor of Divinity degree in 1964 and by Lebanon Valley College with a Doctor of Humane Letters degree in 1965.

During the ten years of his leadership in the Eastern Area of the Evangelical United Brethren Church, he was able to lead the six conferences in redrawing their boundaries to form two conferences with larger resources for more effective ministry. When the United Methodist Church was formed in 1968, Bishop Kaebnick continued to live in Harrisburg, and before retiring in 1972, had the former Evangelical United Brethren and Methodist conferences united.

Bishop Kaebnick has always been a hard worker, an efficient executive able to handle a multitude of details without losing an objective overview or perspective that gave wholeness to his task. His mastery of detail especially qualified him for preparing a workable index of the Discipline which he did each quadrennium.

In looking back over 50 years in the ministry, he said: "The church of Christ is not having an easy time these days. It never has had. It will always have a difficult time so long as it is true to its duty. Its advance is challenged by all the forces of evil from without and by a lot of spiritual sloth within. The leading

symbol of our Christian faith is not an easy chair, but a cross
. . . .

"As for the future, I am not so discouraged. . . . To be sure, complacency is out of order . . . there are resources adequate for every demand that life makes upon us. . . . And though I am an old man, I share at least the hopeful spirit of the young, facing life, as Lowell sang with 'the rays of morn on their white Shields of Expectancy!"

The bishop had all his books, personal items and household goods packed and ready for moving on his day of retirement when Hurricane Agnes caused the Susquehanna River to rise so far beyond flood stage that it submerged the first floor of his home. He lost his library, all his records and "all of the priceless memorabilia" of his wife.

His daughter, Winifred, lost all her lecture notes, bibliographies, syllabi, drafts of thesis and more than five-hundred textbooks related to work toward her Doctor of Philosophy degree. This was a severe blow, but true to her character and like her father, she was not defeated.

Bishop Kaebnick and his daughter moved to 65 Woodbine Drive, Hershey, Pennsylvania, after retirement. His son, Dr. Warren Kaebnick, lives in Troy, Ohio.

Bishop Kaebnick's kind and gracious ways and his dedication to whatever responsibilities have been assigned to him have left a deep imprint upon all who have worked with him. His life and ministry have been a challenge to others.

NOTE

Biographical information provided by H. W. Kaebnick for the author (November 3, 1972).

BISHOP W. MAYNARD SPARKS

17

He Preached
From His Father's Pulpit

When asked about the the influences that led him into the ministry, W. Maynard Sparks replied, "There was no dramatic called to the ministry. I grew up in a parsonage home. I loved my parents and caught something of their love for their calling as pastor and pastor's wife."

After a pause he said, "As I reflect upon the forces that awakened my boyhood mind to the claims of the Christian ministry, there are three experiences that come to mind. First, in World War I years I became a tither, a regular reader of the Holy Scriptures and made a covenant with God to be in prayer daily. To these pledges I affixed my name. These became lifetime commitments. Such I cannot separate from my obedience to the call of the ministry.

"Second, the influence of a parsonage home, dedicated parents, brother and sister, along with the confidence many lay persons placed in me, were strong, positive factors. At the age of 12, my father gave me opportunity to preach one evening in one of his evangelistic meetings. Other invitations came. These brought encouragement."

The third experience he considers to be a factor in pointing him toward the ministry was association with District Superintendent James S. Fulton, who was a frequent visitor to the parsonage home. "As a pastor to a youth in one of his parsonages, he gave the kind of encouragement that brought about my quarterly conference license to preach November 1, 1919, and my permanent license on September 1, 1923, just as I was about to enter Lebanon Valley College."[1]

Walden Maynard Sparks was born in Rockwood, Pennsylvania, December 16, 1906, where his father, The Reverend George Alonzo Sparks was pastor of the United Brethren Church. His father and mother, Sarah Heefner Sparks, spent 38 years in the active ministry of the United Brethren Church in Pennsylvania.

Maynard said, "My boyhood experiences were those of a normal boy. . . . inquiring, experimenting, bypassing at times what my parents wanted me to be and to do. I idolized my father as the preacher and under his preaching and at his invitation I answered to a summons to accept Christ as my Savior in Bigler, Pennsylvania. I attended all church services and at times walked with my father to services at his other appointments. . . . While in high school, I was put in charge of a Sunday school class of young people, some of whom were older in years than I."[2]

Four years at Lebanon Valley College gave him a Bachelor of Arts degree in 1927 and three years in Bonebrake (now United) Theological Seminary earned him a Bachelor of Divinity degree. He was ordained an elder by Bishop Grant D. Batdorf in 1930 and assigned to Sewickley, Pennsylvania, where he lived with one of the families of the church. The next year he was transferred to the Shanksville and Central City churches. He and Blanche May Frank were married October 27, 1931.

After six years at Shanksville and Central City churches, he was appointed to the First United Brethren Church in Punxsutawney where he also served as district leader for the surrounding churches. In 1940, he went to First Church in Wilkinsburg. Lebanon Valley honored him with a Doctor of Divinity degree in 1942.

The Allegheny Conference called him to be superintendent in 1946, a position he held until going to Lebanon Valley College as assistant professor of religion in 1950. He was named chaplain in 1953.

He summarized his pastoral ministry by listing the following areas which received special emphasis: "(1) The teaching ministry of the local church, calling for continued training of leaders, (2) A preaching program that included series of sermons based on Biblical characters and events, (3) pastoral care by going to people, searching for their needs, patiently developing rapport and mutual confidence, (4) relating the local church program to the annual conference and denominational objectives, (5) concern for post-high school educational programs of youth, (6) participating in interdenominational activities, (7) seeking to win men, women and youth to Christ through personal and mass evangelism and help them grow through study and experience for development in the grace and knowledge of the Lord Jesus Christ and (8) finding young men for the Christian ministry. . . ."[3]

Taking to the college campus the same dedication and discipline he demonstrated as pastor, he wrote, "The chaplain seeks to understand the communities of learning and faith . . . deeply concerned that the academic community in its responsibility to

103

the household of faith is constantly true to its vocation . . . is concerned with a pastoral ministry for the whole person within the academic community. . . . Like the pastor of a parish, the college chaplain needs a discerning mind and a shepherd heart. . . . The church college does not have a religious program. It is a religious program."[4]

The 1958 General Conference elected Chaplain Sparks to serve as bishop with residence in Sacramento, California. In 1966, his alma mater honored its distinguished alumnus with Doctor of Humane Letters degree. University of Puget Sound conferred on him the Doctor of Laws degree in 1971. He received a Doctor of Divinity degree from Westmar College in 1973.

Because of the geographical expanse of his ten-state area and the necessity of making many trips to headquarters in Dayton, Ohio, Bishop Sparks was often on the road four or five weeks at a time. When urged to make more trips home between meetings, he said it would put a financial burden on the church and he could not in good conscience do that to the church he loved.

His mail was forwarded to him regularly, and it was not unusual for him to spend entire days in a hotel answering his correspondence, yet he always found time to write a friendly note to some father or mother telling them he had seen their son or daughter. It is no surprise that he is so loved and respected.

Bishop Sparks's overseas assignments took him to Sierra Leone, West Africa, six times to preside over the conference, and to Canada, Europe and Brazil to help prepare the way for union with the Methodist Church.

The bishop's writings have been limited for the most part to church papers and Sunday school literature. He contributed a chapter on the sacraments for the study of the Confession of Faith and two chapters in the book, *Christian Faith Encounters Communism*. Before election as bishop, he served as recording secretary of two General Conferences. With Bishop H. W. Kaebnick, he edited and indexed the 1963 and 1967 Evangelical United Brethren Church Disciplines.

Bishop Sparks has disciplined his ministry to guidelines established early in life, using the early morning hours for meditation, reading, study and writing. It has been his policy to read some books that make heavy demands on the reader. When on the road, he often read in libraries where he had access to dictionaries and encyclopedias. He planned more for a day than he could do. He said, "Nothing motivates me so strongly as the unfinished work at the end of the day. It argues for the need of tomorrow."[5]

He outlines his pattern in sermon preparation, as follows: "(1) Assessing the need that occasions the message, (2) searching the Scriptures and other resources for understanding the Scriptural and contemporary circumstances calling for the message that is being prepared, (3) reading and gathering materials to 'illuminate the subject,' and setting boundary lines, to go where one needs to go and avoid detours. Then comes the writing and rewriting, with those who will be hearing in mind."

He writes, "I have always sought to major in 'feeding the sheep' in pulpit, in pastoral care, in finding and cultivating leadership and in making the institution a living witness. These objectives in the pastorate did not basically change in the episcopacy. Only the dimensions of opportunity were larger."[6]

With union of The Evangelical United Brethren Church and The Methodist Church, Bishop Sparks was assigned to Seattle. Following the death of Bishop Palmer on January 5, 1971, the Oregon-Idaho Annual Conference and the Alaska Mission were added to his area of responsibility.

The bishop's breadth and depth of theological knowledge and perspective, and his ability to articulate his faith in contemporary language has gained for him the respect of scholars. He is thorough in his work, exacting in details, dependable in every responsibility, dedicated and humble in spirit.

Upon retirement in 1972, Bishop and Mrs. Sparks moved back to Sacramento at 5401 Cabrillo Way. He maintains a discipline of daily thirty-minute walks before breakfast, a regular study schedule and one day a week, a visit to city library in the morning and the state library in the afternoon. "I carry my lunch and go to a nearby park to sit with the unemployed and others who come to play checkers and eat their lunch. . . . I never had a sabbatical. . . . Perhaps what I am trying to do now is the nearest to it."[7]

A seminary professor said: "Bishop W. Maynard Sparks has impressed me very deeply as one of the most committed per-

105

After fifty years in the Christian ministry, Paul M. Herrick wrote, "My chief emphasis and first love in the ministry has always been the pastoral work, both when a pastor and a bishop"[1]

A member of his congregation said, "He was at his best when he was near to and serving the people of his congregation and community. He loved people and they loved him. He was a good preacher. His sermons were practical and responded to people's problems and needs."[2]

Another described him as "honest, simple and obedient to Christ as a servant. Paul Herrick shared the joys and hopes of the Christian faith with people of all walks of life. The Scriptures and other great literature were a living part of his mind and spirit."[3]

Paul Murray Herrick was born in the United Brethren Church parsonage at Scandia, Kansas, on April 3, 1898. His father, the Reverend Philo M. Herrick, was one of the pioneer United Brethren ministers in Kansas, where he served for 55 years. His mother, Alice Mary McKee Herrick, was the daughter of the Reverend Joseph McKee, who brought his family into Kansas in 1873.[4]

When Paul was seven, the family moved to a farm near Topeka, Kansas, which had been purchased from the Reverend Mr. Williams, a Free Methodist minister. For several months the two families, each with eight children, lived together in the nine-room stone house.[5] During revival meetings at the Pleasant Hill United Brethren Church, four miles away, nine of the children were converted. Three of the Herrick girls later served as missionaries in the United Brethren schools in New Mexico. Three of the Herrick boys became ministers in the United Brethren Church. Paul was one of them.[6]

In the fall of 1917, he enrolled in Kansas City University, but when the following summer came, he enlisted in the Army. With the signing of the Armistice on November 11, 1918, he was discharged in December and returned to school in the fall of 1919. On June 7, 1922, he was graduated from Kansas City University, and that same day he married Ruth Porter.

During his senior year in the university, Paul decided to become a minister and in February was assigned to serve as student pastor of two churches in Missouri near Polo and

Brookfield. The next two years were spent in serving rural churches and teaching school. In August of 1924, he enrolled in Bonebrake (now United) Theological Seminary. Upon graduation three years later, the family returned to Missouri where Paul was ordained and appointed by the Board of Missions to serve as superintendent of the Missouri Conference. He was only twenty-nine at the time, the youngest minister to serve as superintendent in the United Brethren Church.

He asked for an appointment to a local church in 1929 and was assigned to Stillwater, Oklahoma. Two years later he was appointed to Enid. While leading this congregation through the depression years, he also served as dean of the Summer Bible Conference[7] and did graduate work at Phillips University, receiving a Master of Arts degree.[8] He became pastor of the Otterbein United Brethren Church in Topeka, Kansas, in 1935. York College honored Pastor Herrick with a Doctor of Divinity degree in 1937.[9]

Doctor Herrick became pastor of First United Brethren Church, Dayton, Ohio, in 1941 and gave seventeen and a half years of outstanding leadership to this historic and influential congregation. When he became bishop in 1958, he was to continue living in Dayton to supervise the area in which he had served and was so well known and respected by his fellow ministers.[10] Otterbein College awarded Bishop Herrick an honorary Doctor of Laws degree in 1960.[11]

When the Evangelical United Brethren Church and The Methodist Church united in 1968, Bishop Herrick was transferred to Richmond, Virginia. He and Mrs. Herrick moved into the episcopal manse in August of that year. "I shall never cease to be grateful to these great Virginia people," he said, "and indeed to the Southeastern Jurisdiction for their kind and gracious spirit to us."[12]

Upon his request, he was granted retirement because of deteriorating health in December, 1970. Bishop Herrick wrote: "We secured a house in Dayton, Ohio, and moved back to our favorite city where we had lived for twenty-seven-years. . . . I have done considerable preaching for men on vacation and a seven-months part-time supply at the Fletcher, Ohio, Church.[13]

Free from the exacting schedule of an active bishop, he improved in health and so did his wife. "God has been so good

BISHOP PAUL W. MILHOUSE

19

I Would Do It Again

(*Written by J. Gordon Howard*)

Speaking to an assembly of young people at Oklahoma City University in the fall of 1974, Bishop Milhouse challenged them to consider the Christian ministry as a life-time vocation. His personal enthusiasm for the ministry is reflected in his closing words: "Forty-seven years ago, I took the first step leading me into the ministry. If I had the opportunity to live my life over, I would do it again."

Preaching has always held a central place in the ministry of Paul W. Milhouse. When a gentleman suggested he reduce his preaching schedule, he turned to his secretary after the gentleman left and said, "I wouldn't have this job if I couldn't preach."

His manner of preaching is conversational but convincing. His sermons are biblically based and packed with the fruit of careful study and preparation. His dedication to the pulpit ministry is reflected in this quotation which he had on his pulpit in Decatur, Illinois, "No man can give at one and the same time the impression that he himself is clever and that Jesus Christ is mighty to save."

At a district meeting in a small church in Western Nebraska, a young man approached Bishop Milhouse, shook his hand and looked him over carefully. After a moment of silence, the young man said, "I heard a bishop was coming. I've never seen a bishop, so I came over to see what one looks like."

Paul Milhouse was something of a novelty when he assumed the episcopal office of the Oklahoma Area of the United Methodist Church in 1968, but he was not a novitiate in that office. Already he had served eight years as bishop of the extensive Southeastern Area of the Evangelical United Brethren Church where he had a reputation as a wise churchman, a strong administrator and a tireless worker. For him, the official motto of the State of Oklahoma seemed most appropriate: "Labor conquers all things."

He was the first new bishop seen in 24 years by 270,000 Oklahoma United Methodists. His predecessor, Bishop W. Angie Smith, had enjoyed a long and influential career and was the living symbol of Methodism in Oklahoma for nearly a quarter of a century. What would be the impact of the new bishop on the more than 500 pastors in over 700 churches, and on the more than 50 ministers under special appointment?

Because he is a creative thinker and a diligent worker, Paul Milhouse has found time to write. In the years from 1946 to 1968 there were the following publications: *Enlisting and Developing Church Leaders,* 1946; *Come Unto Me,* 1946; *Except the Lord Build the House,* 1949; *Doorways to Spiritual Living,* 1950; *Lift Up Your Eyes,* 1955; *Christian Worship in Symbol and Ritual,* 1953; *Laymen in the Church,* 1957; *At Life's Crossroads,* 1959; *Facing Frontiers* (editor), 1960; *Life of Philip William Otterbein,* 1968. In his writing Paul Milhouse expresses himself clearly. Much religious writing is ponderous and obscure. Milhouse readers find his writing inspiring, interesting and easy to understand.

In 1950 at the General Conference in Dayton, he was elected associate editor of *The Telescope-Messenger,* official weekly journal of the Evangelical United Brethren Church. In 1954 he was re-elected to this office, and also for two years he assisted with certain church school publications. In addition to his editorial work, he served five years as pastor of Grace Church in nearby Steelton to provide the small congregation with pastoral care.

The General Conference of 1958, in Harrisburg, elected Paul Milhouse as executive secretary of the General Council of Administration. This agency held comprehensive and influential place in the denominational life, and it placed the executive secretary at the center of a vast web of activities reaching into every annual conference and local church.

At this point in time, the Evangelical United Brethren Church was beginning to consider seriously the possibility of union with The Methodist Church, so all phases of church work had to consider the immediate on-going program of the denomination, and at the same time look ahead to a new set of conditions if union with the Methodists should be consummated. But, as expected, Paul Milhouse performed his duties with a wise head and a firm hand.

On the night of Sunday, May 13, 1960, Bishop Lyle L. Baughman, episcopal leader of the Southwestern Area of the Evangelical United Brethren Church, while traveling to the annual session of the Oklahoma-Texas Conference, was stricken with a heart attack and died before medical aid could be summoned. According to Evangelical United Brethren law, it became necessary to elect a new bishop by mail ballot, the voters being the delegates to the 1958 General Conference. In

November, 1960, Paul W. Milhouse was elected bishop and moved to Kansas City. It was necessary, without preparation, to step midstream into the current of his predecessor's administrative program. For this difficult assignment the new bishop proved to be well qualified. He immediately demonstrated to his Area and to the denomination that his election was a wise move on the part of the church.

At this time there were six other active bishops. Bishop Milhouse joined this episcopal fraternity and immediately won the respect and affection of his colleagues. Frequently he was given assignments which required considerable study and research. He always reported on time with his work well done.

The Southwestern Area, except for the Western Area, was the largest in the denomination in terms of geographical expanse. It covered the states of Iowa, Kansas, Missouri, Nebraska, Oklahoma and Texas, which was more square miles than many of the nations of the world. To administrate this Area required much travel, usually by automobile, and involved much physical strain. Three of Bishop Milhouse's predecessors died "on the road," Bishop Arthur B. Stratton, Bishop Victor O. Weidler and Bishop Lyle L. Baughman.

It was not an easy time to be a bishop of The Evangelical United Brethren Church. The whole denomination was caught up in the prospect of union with The Methodist Church. Bishop Milhouse kept all aspects of the work of his Area functioning effectively, and at the same time prepared the way for church union. When the vote was taken on church union, the Southwestern Area was one of the most favorable to uniting with the Methodists.

In Dallas in May, 1968, The Methodist Church and The Evangelical United Brethren Church, after all legal steps had been taken and with appropriate ceremonies, became The United Methodist Church with approximately 11,000,000 members. In this new ecclesiastical structure Bishop Milhouse was assigned to the South Central Jurisdiction and to the Oklahoma Area.

Something of the Milhouse philosophy of administration is revealed in a statement he made to a fellow bishop: "We maintain a rather flexible staff relationship in our conference. I seldom make specific assignments to my administrative assis-

117